An Unconventional Life

An Unconventional Life Jonathan Clift

AN UNCONVENTIONAL LIFE

ISBN: 978-1-4457-7939-3

Design by John Amy at Promo Design
www.promo-design.co.uk

Contents

Mark

JUST as the first dusky pink blossom appeared on a straggly tree outside the Inn I turned seventeen. My life was made up of numbers: seventeen years, the year 1956 and twenty long miles from the nearest decent town, Cheltenham. I'd spent the last sixteen years exhausting every walk in the Cotswold Hills and I yearned for adventure, but not much happens in the middle of nowhere.

My best friend Mark was as bored as I was, so we hatched a naïve teenage plan. We would find a hobby, improve our bodies and our prospects with the local girls. Every Thursday night we'd head to a barn in the next village, I'd be the passenger on the crossbar of Mark's bike, heading for the gymnastics class. I didn't have a bike so each week Mark would make the journey to the Inn, where I lived with my parents. The Inn was a large bar, mainly frequented by locals, with a few rooms attached for passing trade and people on walking holidays. It was known for two things: Somerset cider and Mother's wonderful home-cooked meals.

Each evening she'd disappear into the kitchen and tempt any guests down the stairs with home-made chicken pie or faggots with soft dumplings floating in delicious gravy.

We'd freewheel down the slope out of the village to class. It was run by two brothers who were training the entire class to put on a show at the village fete.

I had a crucial role in the show. As the smallest gymnast in the class they wanted me to be at the top of a human pyramid. It was to be the climax of the show. At fifteen I'd stopped growing, at just 5ft 3 inches. Compared to the lads around me I was puny. With blonde hair and blue eyes I knew I'd never be the latin lover the ladies wanted. But my looks made me the focus on that day. It arrived too quickly and I stood poised, the star attraction, an unbalanced tree-top decoration on a very shaky set of branches. I could feel the collapse before I saw it and I ended up doing a rather spectacular swan dive into the arms of the safety catchers. I was fine. Unfortunately for my saviour my arm crunched into to his nose, breaking it in several places. As he lay on the grass, with a crowd gathering and several helpers shoving plugs of cotton wool up his nose, it suddenly dawned on me that gymnastics might not be my calling. So after about five minutes' consideration Mark and I decided that the only hobby worth taking up was girls.

As athletic young lads we thought we'd be totally irresistible to the opposite sex. Mark eventually got a girlfriend called Clare and I managed to land a girlfriend, Jane, but any attempts at seduction were met with slaps and a painful knee in the groin. I was hoping Mark might have a few handy hints but it turned out that he was faring no better. It looked like I'd be as useless in love as I was in gymnastics.

Clare and Mark's relationship was volatile from the beginning. She was short-tempered and Mark would just make things worse by teasing her when she got mad. She was good looking but in a tomboyish way, tall for a girl with short dark hair. She was constantly looking for adventure and had made it clear to Mark that she wanted to join the Army after school. Their relationship was never destined to be a great love story, rather they were just playing out roles of a teenage relationship, doing what was expected of a girl and boy of their age, but both enjoying the platonic friendship they had.

My Jane was a girly girl. Blonde, petite with a happy-go-lucky attitude. We were best friends, she was my confidante, my listener, but we knew we had no future. I knew I wanted to be in the RAF and she knew she wanted to be a nurse. While our friends talked about settling down, marriage and children we focussed on dancing and having fun.

I'd known Mark as far back as I could remember, he grew up four miles from me, the youngest of three lads, both his brothers already married with children. As the years passed Mark transformed into the kind of guy that women swoon over: tall, dark hair and green eyes with a strong build and pleasant, kind personality. It amazed me he'd turned into such a gentle soul because his parents made no secret of the fact they were keen to bundle Mark off so they could get on with their own life.

Mark's parents met at a dance when they were both nineteen and married 6 years later. His father worked on the railway, a good steady job he was happy to work the rest of his life in, and his mother did a few hours in the kitchen of a local school but spent most of her time looking after his two older brothers and Mark.

Dance was their passion, a string of babysitters ensured they could spend as much time as possible on the floor. Mark loved the things his parents loved: dance, football (like his dad) and pleasing his mum. Keeping Mum happy was important. When he eventually got into grammar school his mum told all the neighbours he was going to be an architect; poor Mark had no idea what he wanted to do. Undeterred, his mother saved every penny she could to send Mark to college to fulfil 'his dream'.

Jane, my ever-tolerant girlfriend, and Clare, the now-constant companion to Mark, talked us into joining a dance club. Each Wednesday we'd trek over to Mark's village and every Saturday we'd get the coach to dances in other villages. We'd spend hours dancing to upcoming local bands. At the end of the night there was always one snag, the coach would drop us off near Mark's house at about 1am. We'd walk the girls back and then I had a four-mile slog back home. No street lights meant I was at the mercy of the moonlight.

Week after week I made the journey, convinced someone was following me, jumping at odd noises and the patterned reflections made by the branches of the trees. My parents became so concerned about my jittery state that they were the ones to suggest Mark walk home with me after the Saturday night dance and sleep over. Then the next week I'd sleep at Mark's.

I loved staying there. He had all the modern conveniences that the Inn wouldn't see for a few more years, indoor plumbing and central heating. It was bliss: no running across a freezing cold yard in the middle of the night just for a pee, or facing the gross contents of the chamber pot. Our idea of a bath was Mother filling a jug with water from the kettle, boiled on the stove, and poured into the old tin bath.

By the time we'd get to Mark's his parents were snoring. He'd always offer to pour me a drink, usually a foul-tasting whisky that would linger on my breath for hours. The last thing I wanted was to offend my best mate so I'd swig back the amber medicine, feeling my head spinning. We'd sleep in his small room, sparse with its one double bed and a wardrobe.

I'd always slept alone so sharing a room with my friend was exciting, like camping in an exotic location, and I enjoyed the closeness without knowing why. That first night I fell asleep instantly, warmed by the whisky and close body. Sunday morning gave away smells of crisping bacon. Washing my pounding head in the clean and modern bathroom I felt a slap on my rear. 'Let's get some breakfast, slowcoach,' Mark joked, in a jovial way that was so much part of who he was. 'I want you to meet my parents.'

Over eggs sunny side up we chatted about Mark's study as an architect. I was running a small poultry farm and I had no idea the following days would change the direction of both of our lives. Just a few days later a formal letter arrived at the Inn; it was my call to do National Service. Mother dropped into instant panic, what did I know about life outside a village, how would I cope? I knew it was my escape route and I couldn't wait to tell Mark.

Dance night arrived and I was buzzing at the prospect of telling my best mate about my impending exit into the real world. His subdued reaction shocked me. 'So when do you go?' he mumbled into his chest. Initially I didn't register his reaction. 'A few weeks, great news, isn't it? I'll finally get out of this dull village!' Mark wouldn't raise his eyes to meet me.

Confused by Mark's reaction I went to Jane, where I found kisses and consolation until the end of the night. My walk home with Mark to the Inn that night felt tense, the looming shadows cast darkness around his hooded eyes and he remained silent. Sitting in the bar I poured whisky and we talked girlfriends and what the next few months would bring. Mark's mood began to lift and we talked through half a bottle of spirits.

Unsteady on our feet we helped each other to my ground floor rooms, freezing because of the French doors that led to the garden. 'How can you stand this temperature?' exclaimed Mark. Laughing at him hopping round the room to keep warm I was hysterical by the time he'd leapt in and out of the cold linen sheets.

'There's no way I'm sleeping alone in that ice box.' He huddled up beside me in my single bed. 'It might get a bit cramped in here,' I pleaded. But it was obvious he was going nowhere. Gradually we both stopped shivering. I could feel Mark breathing on my neck, each exhalation tickling the hairs. I could feel Mark moving in closer and his hand start to move down my body, his fingertips reached the front of my shorts. 'What the hell are you doing?' I hissed. Saying nothing he took hold of my hand and placed it gently inside his pants. My brain fought against shame but it felt good and I wanted the feeling to continue. We'd crossed a line.

A tap on the door woke us the next morning: Mother standing there with a tray of tea and a shocked expression was enough to bring Mark from his hiding place under the eiderdown. Keen to explain away what had happened I blamed the cold and draughty room. 'I hope you slept well, Mark, it must have been a little cramped in there, but you boys don't seem to mind roughing it at your age,' Mother said with an approving half-grin.

Thinking we'd passed the test we dressed and made our way down to the warm kitchen, only to find test two: Father at the gnarled kitchen table, his hands resting on the unopened Sunday newspaper. He glanced over at Mark, waiting for the dark-haired intruder to introduce himself. I felt miles away as I used the kitchen cabinet for support, hoping they would find some common ground.

They did – cars. Mark offered to take a look at Dad's clapped-out old Ford after breakfast. 'It's kind of you to offer,' said Father. I was more than a little impressed, as I had no idea he had any knowledge about cars. It turned out he'd spent many summer evenings tinkering with cars in his father's garage. Breakfast and cars were the only topics for discussion over toast and home made marmalade and endless cups of tea; no mention of the bed-sharing catch out. I'd already decided it wouldn't be something I'd talk to Mark about. It was just a one-off, not to be repeated, especially when my report letter arrived a few days later.

My parents didn't have the most romantic of starts, meeting at my great aunt's funeral. Father was the hearse driver, working to pay his way through college to become a banker. Mother, a beautiful twenty-one-year-old training at catering college, winked at Father as they returned from the service. 'Nice job you've got there,' she smirked. 'It's only temporary till I have enough money to take you out,' said Father, smiling broadly.

A few nights later they had their first date and quickly fell into an intense relationship. Mother started working in a smart restaurant under the guidance of a famous chef and had big plans to open her own place. But just a year later Mother found out she was pregnant with me, ruining her career prospects and prompting a hastily arranged wedding at the local registry office.

They managed to scrap together enough money for a

honeymoon in Penzance and then waited for me to make my entrance. And what an entrance it turned out to be. I was born at home by forceps; my forehead still bears the mark of where they penetrated my skin. But I came out silent and still so the doctor, thinking I was stillborn, put me to one side. My aunt decided that simply wasn't good enough and picked me up, massaging me briskly in front of the fire. Just seconds later I apparently let out a huge scream and peed all over the doctor.

I remember as a young child watching my father go off to work in the bank but he never seemed particularly content with his job, only with his home life. Over the next few years, and with no more children appearing, they built up a pot of money. So when the chance came to buy a business, the Inn, my mother pushed Father hard. She wanted to be tenant and Father wanted Mother to be happy.

Father gave his job up at the bank and became pint-puller. Mother concentrated on cooking, something that would bring people in from miles around. I became an important part of the Inn, acting as delivery boy at Christmas, as we acted as pub and local off-licence. I stashed my wages away and used them to start my little poultry farm at fourteen. By the time I was ready to leave on National Service I'd saved up six pounds.

I had to go to Liverpool Street Station to join the other lads in my intake. We'd travel to Wilmslow in Cheshire to do our basic training. As Saturday night seemed to be the night for revelations I told Mark I was due to leave. 'Ok, how about we go for a few days away?' he suggested positively. 'Great, we could invite the girls,' I replied, thinking he'd love that idea. There was no way I wanted the girls there and by the look on Mark's face, neither did he. As he took off his clothes and moved across to my bed I knew we'd moved from playing around to something real.

'Cold again last night?' questioned Mother as she cracked open the door. Winking, she left the steaming tea on the side. 'Now we'll have to get engaged,' jibed Mark. As funny as the situation was we were both worried that Mother would tell all and Mark would be pushed out. I knew his own family was plagued by insecurity and disagreements and I wanted him to be liked and feel love. But we had nothing to worry about. Over crumpets and bacon Father greeted Mark like a long lost friend: 'Don't know what you did to that car of mine but it's been running beautifully.'

I was due to leave at the end of June, so the weekend before we set off on our camping trip. As the country roads passed us by I felt calm enough to talk to Mark about what had happened between us. 'Do you think I'm gay?' I asked. Mark grinned. 'I don't know about that, John. What I do know is that when I'm with you it feels natural and so it can't be wrong.' 'Maybe it's just a phase we're going through...' Just as quickly we moved on to talking about Mark's football team and the subject was dropped.

We arrived at the most beautiful lake, surrounded by water

lilies in delicate shades of pink. Tucked away from the main roads, on the edge of Dartmoor, the banks of the lake were covered with purple wild flowers. Mark pitched the tent and I collected wood, lit a fire and opened wine.

The rays of the sun were shimmering off the lake and I knew it would be an ideal day to row out into the middle of the lake to fish. It was stocked with fresh water trout and as the day lazily slipped by we contemplated doing nothing except spending time together.

We caught freshwater fish we thought would make a good meal. The pure taste of the lake remained on the fish when they were grilled and as the sun dipped behind the lake we felt for our future. 'I'm going to be an architect, you know, it'll happen,' he said softly. 'I want to be an interior designer,' I replied, 'just not sure what Mother and Father would make of that.' 'You've got to chase your dreams, John – what else is there in life?'

The second bottle of wine was the catalyst for a swim. Collecting our towels we stripped off and ran naked into the warm water. Swimming far from the lily-covered edges it was a moon-filled paradise.

Suddenly I felt a strong current pulling me down. I went under and I knew I was in trouble. I called to Mark for help and as I was going down for the third time he grabbed my arm. Dragging me to the edge of the lake I was aware he was trying to get me out of the water and give me the kiss of life.

'Thank God for that! I thought I'd lost you.' Mark looked

into my eyes, tears streaming from his own. He tried to get me to my feet but I couldn't walk, shocks of cold were smashing through my legs and arms. Gently lifting me, Mark carried me to our tent, covering me in layers of soft blankets and his own warmth until I stopped shaking. The smell of warm canvas and the weight of my best friend's arm roused me the next day. He'd saved my life.

The following week I prepared to leave my sheltered life and enter the real world. I didn't see Mark for a few days, which I thought was strange. The last night I went to bed early. I was firm asleep when I heard a tap on my window. I thought at first it was the storm which had become very wild. There was a flash of lightning and standing outside was Mark.

I opened the French doors to let him in. He was absolutely drenched. 'Come in, you're mad coming out in this weather. Take off your things, I can loan you a shirt and some shorts,' I whispered. Mark stripped off his clothes and before I could reach for some replacements he jumped into my bed. I wanted to know where he had been all week. 'I had to go away, bad timing I know, but I couldn't let you leave without saying goodbye,' said Mark.

That time I didn't hesitate about sleeping with Mark, I had no doubts. The next day I woke up to find he had gone, leaving his cross and chain and a note which read 'keep safe'.

Mother was in a strange mood at breakfast, she asked if

Mark had slept in my room last night. I said that he had, but she couldn't understand why he didn't stay for breakfast. What I didn't know was that she was about to tell my father. 'You know Mark stayed here last night,' said Mother. 'Well, yes, he stays all the time,' replied Father. Mother then explained she thought we were having an affair. 'Don't be silly, Mother. John's not gay and Mark likes football and cars.'

With a flick of his newspaper he ended the conversation. Muttering into the pages he said, 'Well, he's off to the RAF today so that'll sort things out.' Mother stared hard at the paper barrier and whispered, 'Whatever people do never changes the way they are.'

The RAF

My first weeks in the RAF were like a holiday, which is more than could be said for the majority of the lads. Most of them were already ticking off the days until their release. I thought they were mad. I was enjoying everything. I even relished camping out on moors, six to a small tent and washing in the river which bought back memories of my holiday at the lake with Mark. Despite my size I was athletic and played lots of sport, giving me an advantage over some of my less hardy and more bloated airman mates.

I threw myself into the endurance tests, keen to prove myself as one of the lads. Military life and its routine suited me. I soon got sent to Hereford where I learnt to be part of the stores procedure team and as soon as I passed my examinations for trade training, I found myself posted to Germany.

My introduction to Germany was stormy. Crossing the channel by boat we sailed in a force ten gale. I was one of the last six airmen to board, only to be told there were no more bunks for us to sleep in and we'd have to spend the night on the wooden seats in the dining area with our kit bags as pillows. I spent the whole night lying as still as possible on a bench as hard as concrete, listening to people vomit all around me.

The scene greeting us at the Hook of Holland was just as depressing: was snowing and freezing cold. Most of the lads were fed up, still suffering from that night which seemed like hell to most of them. I thought they were wimps, it would take more than a night on a boat in a rough sea to depress me. I was posted to a town called Celle, near Hanover, starting in the main stores and quickly moving to sort out a sub store with 145 Squadron.

I wanted to fill my days, so when the officers announced they were having tennis trials to find two airmen to join the senior ranks in the station tennis team, I signed up. Thirty airmen turned up to try out and I thought I wouldn't stand a chance. Round after round I knocked my opponents out and finally won a coveted place on the team.

The night before my first tournament I sat in my barracks, stringing a new racket and reading a letter from Mark.

Expecting news of home I was startled by his request. He wanted me to be his best man. He was twenty by now, and both his brothers were married with children, so I guess he didn't want to be the odd one out. I'd presumed once I'd got back from the RAF that we'd pick up where we left off, I didn't think he'd move on so quickly. I had no idea that he was interested in marriage, I thought the last thing he wanted was a woman. How wrong I was – for the first time in my life I felt rejected and hurt.

I'd never really understood what Mark had seen in me. I'd always thought that men saw something in me that gave off a strange vibe but I didn't think I was effeminate. As a teenager I'd always imagined that I would be married by my mid-twenties. Now, as Mark announced his impending marriage by letter, I was beginning to think it would never happen to me. Sleeping with Mark had made me ask all sorts of questions. Did my blonde hair and blue eyes and small stature make me attractive to gay men? I never got the same sexual vibes from girls. I found it so difficult to understand how Mark could so easily change his orientation. All those nights we spent together surely must have meant something to him.

I was the only Other Rank in the tennis team and I soon formed a close friendship with my partner, a Dental Officer called Joe Court. I thought it very unusual that he let me call him Joe when we were alone. Officers were not supposed to get familiar with Other Ranks. I was just a corporal but for some reason I felt there was always warmth in the way he spoke to me, he obviously liked me. We were by far the strongest tennis players on the team. We were so successful he asked me if I would do some tournaments with him. Joe and his fellow officers looked after me, driving the team all over Germany for inter-station matches and smuggling me into the Officers' Mess for tea and cake after the games.

But this started to create jealousy. The other airmen didn't like me being the only airman in the tennis team, and swanning around with the officers, but I wasn't going to let that stop my fun. I was quite happy being the unofficial team mascot.

On our next outing to a match near the Dutch border my enthusiasm couldn't even be dampened by the pouring rain. Speeding down the autobahn, Joe suddenly lost control and we went into a skid, swerving from one side of the road to the other. Crashing into another car I felt the crunch of metal and my side of the car giving way. Smelling petrol I clambered out with the rest of my team mates, only to find Joe trapped by his legs. Bleeding and semi-conscious I took his hand and tried to comfort him, he could hardly stand the pain in his legs. All I wanted to do was get him out of there fast. In that moment I felt a flash of love for Joe, but even in that crazy situation I had to keep how I felt from the other officers or we'd be in deep trouble. Hours passed and we heard that Joe only had minor injuries but I wanted to see him. I borrowed a scooter from another airman and took him a few personal things I thought he would need.

His face lit up when he saw me come through the door to his ward. 'You shouldn't have come all this way to see me,' he said. 'It's no problem,' I replied. He squeezed my hand and felt the affection between us. 'I couldn't let my partner down, could I?' I said, trying hard not to cry. 'Has your wife been to see you?' I asked. He tensed his face. 'No, I'm afraid not, she's probably got more important things to do,' he replied. I thought it very strange.

I sensed there was more to this marriage than I would really want to know. He had a sad look in his eyes when he talked about his wife. I knew she was very attractive, and some airmen made tasteless remarks about her. 'My wife has many hobbies and sits on lots of committees,' he remarked, in a rather unconvincing voice. 'Look, it's not for me to say, but I would have thought you would have come first in her priorities,' I shot back. 'Listen, John, sometimes life is not always what it should be. You have to make allowances, and be as understanding as you can, otherwise relationships just fall apart,' he said. But nothing would convince me that not visiting him was the right thing to do.

'Sorry we had to miss the match,' he said. 'It probably would have been rained off anyway,' I replied. Turning to look at me directly, he said, 'You know I really think we should, at some point, do some tournaments together, just you and I. We have a great partnership.'

I said I'd love to, but was worried about what the other airmen would make of it. Officers weren't supposed to mix and get friendly with Other Ranks. He suggested we take leave at the same time to go and play.

'Wouldn't your wife object, taking leave to play in a tournament?' I asked. 'Don't worry about that, we take separate holidays, and she need never know, we don't discuss what we are doing on leave,' he replied. It seemed a strange marriage to me.

Two weeks later Joe was out of hospital and ready to play tennis again. Just when I thought things were beginning to improve I started hearing terrible rumours, stories of airmen visiting Joe's wife late at night when he was on duty.

I couldn't believe it at first but however hard I tried to ignore the talk, the rumours just got worse and worse. Every moment I was with him I wanted to let him know I supported him in every way possible, but I had no control over this malicious gossip. What was his wife thinking of, cheating on Joe in this way? If only I could tell her how stupid she was. I felt so sorry for Joe but as a junior to him I didn't think I was in a position to tell him, and came to the conclusion that he must know what was happening in his own home.

While I was on holiday in Switzerland Joe was back in England on his own break, arriving back a day before me. I thought it would be good to see him again, and renew our partnership on the tennis court. So I cut my holiday short by a day and as soon as I got back pretended to take a message to the married quarters where he lived with his wife. When I arrived at the front door I heard the most terrible row going on inside. His wife was screaming at the top of her voice.

Turning, I was just about to disappear around the corner when Joe came out of the house and ran towards me. Telling me to keep on walking we went right out of the main gate to the woods. He turned to me. I could see that there were tears in his eyes. 'I'm sorry you had to witness that scene, but as you can gather, things are far from right with my marriage. I need a large drink, but we can't be seen together. If you stay here, I'll get my car and we can drive to the next town.' I knew it wasn't wise to get involved but I just couldn't let Joe down.

We arrived at a small country hotel hidden down back lanes. Joe ordered two double brandies and dry ginger, a drink he called a Horse's Neck. After several of these I realised Joe was on a mission to get totally plastered. When he wasn't looking I took large mouthfuls of water to try to avoid becoming totally incapable. It was clear we weren't going back to the station that night so I asked the barman if they had any single rooms. All they had was a double so I took it.

I had to practically carry Joe to the room. Putting him to bed, all that I could think of was how much trouble we'd be in if someone spotted us. I didn't sleep at all that night, watching the ticking clock and the rise and fall of Joe's chest. In the morning I went down to the breakfast room. Returning with coffee and two croissants I found Joe with his head in his hands. Refusing to eat anything he cradled his coffee.

'Did I make a complete fool of myself last night?'

I told him how drunk he'd been and he apologised over and over. I paid the bill at reception and we returned to the station, completely unnoticed. For the next few months Joe's marriage seemed more stable. What I didn't know was that his wife was pregnant with someone else's child and he'd agreed to stay with her until the birth, then they'd divorce.

Just before the baby was born Joe called me and asked me to play in a tournament in Southern Germany. He told me we'd have to stay in a hotel as it was too far away from our base. So we drove the five hours to the tournament set by a lake. Joe had already booked us into a small hotel, deciding we'd share a room.

It was a very small room with two single beds pushed together in the centre with only just enough room to get into bed either side. 'Cosy, isn't it?' remarked Joe with a smile on his face. I thought it strange that an officer would willingly share with a corporal and I was sure it was against regulations but he was so nice to me I said nothing. We decided to get some practice in and then had a drink in the café. I wanted to know more about his marriage. He said he'd only been married two years but things hadn't been good for some time. Reaching across to squeeze my arm he changed the direction of the conversation, 'There's a welcoming party tonight, let's get ready so we can have a great time, and remember no one knows us here so I'm just Joe.'

Joe was in a great mood at the party, introducing us to all

the other players. Towards the end of the evening he pulled me aside and led me to a quiet bar beside the water and he started to open up about his marriage.

'My marriage went wrong when I came home unexpectedly one night and found her in bed with two airmen, after that it was all downhill. I'm partly to blame because to be honest I never wanted to marry in the first place, but where I live if you haven't got a wife by the time you're twenty five they think there's something wrong with you.'

I wanted to know what he planned to do next. 'I can't go on living as I have been doing so I'll get a divorce when we get back; it's all such a mess.' There was a slight pause and then he continued, 'The only thing that has kept me sane during the past months is having your company and playing tennis with you.' He reached across the table for my hand and looked at me for a moment in the same way Mark had done.

Lying on our beds that night I could feel the sadness coming from Joe.

He suddenly said, 'I had a friend once, we did everything together, we were very close and one night we slept together. In the morning he rode off on his motorbike and was killed by a speeding motorist. I guess I've never really got over it.' There was a long silence as I tried to think of something to say. As I was just about to fall asleep I heard Joe murmur, 'John, would you mind if I came over to join you?' I was stunned, but agreed. He moved over to my bed and we drifted off to sleep wrapped in each other's arms.

As dawn broke the sun cast a surreal light through our window as we lay naked together. Our passion swept over us until we lay motionless, our bodies damp with the exertions of the first light. I wondered if Joe would feel differently after what had happened. Half-running to the shower, a few minutes later I felt his hands on me and no sense of regret.

That afternoon I sat with the sunshine warming my face. My thoughts passed between what had happened with Mark and now with Joe. I had to accept that marriage and children would no longer be a part of my life but I didn't want to let go of what I, and the rest of the world, thought was normal.

I was gay and had to stop pretending otherwise. I'd thought I could explain away my feelings – Mark was just a teenage crush, but the feelings I had for Joe went so much deeper. Each time Joe took me in his arms I knew a truth there was no other way to live. This was who I was and I couldn't stop it. I was willing to face the inevitable pain and disgust from friends and family. Would I be called a fruit or worse? Would my parents really be there for me? Would I be an outcast?

But as quickly as doubts were raised they were extinguished by Joe. He'd hold me and tell me how important I was to him, how full his life was when I was in it. How could I turn away from that?

As the week went by we became totally involved and I couldn't help thinking that other people would notice, whereas Joe just didn't seem to care. We won the tournament and were presented with a huge trophy. Joe wanted to stay another night, saying that he couldn't face going back. 'I'm going to move into the Officers' Mess,' he said. We had no idea how we would see one another but Joe said we would find a way.

We were told that our winning trophy would be placed in a glass case in the Officers' Mess. Joe insisted that we go together to take it there and as we entered a loud cheer went up and all the officers stood up and clapped, it was a time that we would never forget. From that moment on we'd sneak time together when we could. A week at a tennis academy, a present from our Commanding Officer, was a gift to our relationship and we'd hatch plans to drive out to far-flung tennis centres to catch a few hours together.

I was so scared of getting caught that I hadn't considered our relationship could end another way. Joe called me and I could tell by his voice there was something terribly wrong. We met outside the main gate, got into his car and drove to a wood in silence. I felt sick with anticipation and insisted Joe tell me what was wrong. We sat down under a large oak tree. 'I've been posted to the Far East,' said Joe. Instantly weeping I threw my arms around my lover. He told me he would be there for two years and this was the life you chose when you decided on the military. I didn't want to accept what I knew was the truth and although he was sat right beside me I could feel him slipping away.

We managed one last holiday, back at the hotel where we

first made love, swimming in the lake; we lost ourselves in hours of making love. My final goodbye came outside the station gate, Joe handed me the photograph of us with the trophy and promised to keep in touch. My relationship with Joe made me realise a relationship with a woman and marriage wasn't for me. I became reclusive and Joe's letters told the same story. Each day that passed seemed eternal, I didn't want anything or anyone else and I couldn't see when we would ever be together again.

I still played tennis but it didn't feel the same without Joe. One day during practice my new partner told me he wanted a word with me. I asked what it was about and he said that it was obvious that I missed Joe. 'The Commanding Officer knew you two were very close and shared rooms when you were away at training and tournaments. He's asked me to tell you that this is not acceptable, Other Ranks do not share accommodation with officers, it's against regulations and that's why he was posted to the Far East.' I thought this was a pathetic explanation. Did they think parting us would stop us loving each other? Nothing could change the powerful feelings we had for one another.

'We've opened your letters from Joe and we have to insist that there is no further communication between you and him,' he finished.

I felt like I'd been spied on but also like I'd had a lucky escape. Our relationship could have meant a court martial for both of us and if the Commanding Officer hadn't been such a tennis fan it could have been the end of my RAF career. I was desperate to send one last letter to Joe but was told it was impossible. After that incident I noticed the other officers were being extra nice to me and I knew they must know about Joe and me. Soon word spread amongst the other airmen and I became a target, for abuse and the sexual needs of whoever wanted me. I started counting the days until my discharge.

The thought of losing Joe hit me hard. Before I joined the RAF I treated my affair with Mark as a teenage crush. But with Joe, for the first time, I felt a real sense of love and commitment. Joe was risking his career in the forces every time he met me, putting me ahead of his desire to move forward in his job. I felt swept off my feet and for once my feelings had totally overcome any sense of danger or responsibility. Appearing to everyone as tennis partners, the looks between us told another more intimate story. As our love deepened we felt nothing else mattered. We were excited about the way we'd danced around authority. But the excitement was always tempered by the fact we'd get caught out, and it had finally happened. Someone had stepped in to spoil our happiness.

Going home

Two weeks before my return to England I had one more guard duty to do. It was midwinter and freezing cold with snow on the ground. There were four of us in pairs of two and we had to do two hours on and two hours off. On the rest period we were allowed to sleep in the hut which was heated by two pot belly stoves. I was on duty with an airman called Brad from signals, guarding a petrol dump on the edge of the perimeter fence. I wasn't keen on Brad, he was good looking and he knew it and I thought he was a bit of a show-off. After Joe left, he was one of the guys making suggestive comments every time I passed his section.

Our rest period came around and we couldn't wait to get into the hut. We huddled around the stove until we were almost warm and then took off our clothes and got into bed. I must have dropped off to sleep but was woken by Brad next to me, completely naked. I tried to push him out of bed but he was so much stronger than me. 'Why are you resisting? You know you want it,' he whispered. I hit him hard across the mouth. He hit me back harder and I could feel blood running down my face. 'I know about you and that officer, an Other Rank not good enough for you?' He breathed the words into my ear. I knew by then there was no point in struggling anymore unless I wanted to be badly hurt. He ripped down my shorts. It was payback for all the times I had ignored him. He was rough, thrusting inside me. He whispered, 'You'll get more at the next break.' That night I was a wreck with a swollen lip and marks all over my body and I couldn't wait to get back to my room for a shower. The next day I spent curled up in bed. I spent hours just staring at the ceiling, unable to sleep, going over what had happened again and again.

I really didn't know Brad and imagined he'd infected me with a ghastly sexual problem I'd be forced to report to the Medical Officer. In those hours when I burned with anger and shame I tried to figure out why Brad had forced himself on me. I'd never given any indication that I was attracted to him but maybe that was part of the reason. A challenge for him? The whole episode threw my mind into confusion, I could make no sense out of it. There was so much I didn't know about him – maybe he had had serious relationship problems or experiences in his past that had made him act this way. He handled me so crudely, with no affection, and I wondered if he'd been more affectionate would I have welcomed his advances? He wasn't unattractive but he didn't even know for sure that I was gay.

I lay there in my bunk hurting all over and turning things over in my mind. I shouldn't have ignored him when he tried to engage me in conversation all those times. I knew that must have been hurtful. Maybe if I'd talked to him things would have been different? I badly needed friendship after losing Joe – maybe Brad was as desperate as me? I knew what he'd done was wrong but in a twisted way I could understand it – he knew he had to keep his sexuality under the radar and was used to using aggression to get what he wanted.

I eventually got up and took another shower, knowing I couldn't wash away the memory of being raped. My swollen lip had gone down but I felt as if everyone was looking at me when I came out of my room. I had my excuses lined up, I'd say I'd been in a fight, but I wanted to hide away where no one could see me.

I went to the station cinema that evening – it was dark and quiet, a place to hide. I wanted to take my mind off things but after the show I bumped into Brad. I felt sick and started to shake. He was the last person that I wanted to see. 'Hi, I'd like a word with you. Not here though, outside the camp gate,' he said, staring directly at me, with not a hint of apology or regret. I was terrified there would be another confrontation. 'Brad, I just want to go to bed, I'm tired,' I replied, protesting as hard as I could without causing a scene.

'I must speak to you,' he insisted. We walked slowly to the main gate and a short way down the road. He stopped. I wanted to just turn around and make my escape. I threw a punch, hoping to catch him off-guard, but he blocked the blow and held on to my wrists in an iron grip. I felt violated. 'Don't be scared. I just want to say sorry and ask you if you're going to report me, I've been worried all day I never saw you at meals,' he whispered.

'I couldn't eat, I felt sick, after last night,' I replied.

He half-smiled. 'You've got to eat. Anyone would think I'd

tried to kill you.'

I couldn't understand his mix of humour and concern and anger flashed through me.

'Don't worry, I don't plan to write an article in the RAF magazine about your attack on me,' I shouted, hitting him across his face.

For the first time I saw a glimpse of regret cross his face. 'I want to invite you out as an apology,' he said in a sincere voice. 'You don't have to do that. Let's just try to forget it, if that's possible,' I replied. I really felt that after what had happened I would have a hard time trying to be civil to him. I'd grown up in a family where we were taught not to hold grudges so my instinct was to forgive, despite the painful physical and mental scars the night before had left. He refused to take no for answer and he

gently pulled me towards him, kissing me on the cheek.

My stomach churned with hate, and longing and unable to express what I felt I turned and walked away, just relieved he hadn't been aggressive.

That Friday I had a call from Brad, wanting to know if I was off duty over the weekend and telling me to meet him outside the main gate at 6pm. There was no way I could cause a scene about it as I had been warned to keep a low profile on this sort of thing.

I arrived to find Brad leaning against the bonnet of his car. He ordered me into the car and drove silently for two hours. I didn't know whether to be thrilled or terrified. We pulled up outside a mansion-style hotel set by a river. 'I've ordered dinner for 8pm so we'd better take our bags straight up,' barked Brad. In the dining room we found our table overlooking the water. Without even looking at me Brad said, 'Order what you like, it's all on me.' He then proceeded to order a frantically expensive bottle of wine. Once we'd had a glass or two I started to relax and realised he could act like a gentleman, albeit a very abrupt one. As we chatted I realised I knew very little about this enigmatic character as we'd exchanged so few words. Turns out he was a charming host, funny and laid-back and I couldn't quite believe the change in him from that terrible night on guard duty.

We finished our dinner and went up to our room. 'I would like to apologise for the way I acted on guard duty. You don't have to go to bed with me and if you like I'll drive you back to the station right now,' said Brad.

I was taken aback by this total change in his attitude and I knew the last thing on his mind was driving me back to the station. I hadn't quite figured out my next move so suggested we went back to the bar for a few drinks. I knew at this point that Brad must have been desperate when he raped me while we were on guard duty. It was not his normal behaviour. I felt so sorry for him.

He ordered two brandies at the bar. 'The first thing I want to know is why you acted like you did.' He must have been in a confessional mood. 'It may be something to do with my childhood. You see, I was abused by my stepfather for years, he was rough with me and I guess I thought that's the way you behave if you want someone. It happened right up until I came into the Service and then I met one person my own age in Brighton. It's not a lot of experience, is it?' Brad said.

'So you must have had a really unhappy childhood,' I replied. 'You could say that, but I survived.'

I thought at that moment what a different upbringing Brad had to mine. I was so thankful that I had wonderful parents that I could rely on to support me when sometime things were not all that I hoped they'd be.

He asked me about my relationship with Joe and as I explained how deeply we'd become involved I found myself liking Brad more and more.

'You will get nowhere being aggressive to anyone,' I said. 'The other person must be consenting, you're a good looking guy, girls would fall over backwards to go out with you'. He simply grinned and said, 'It's not girls I want, they've two things I don't need and they're missing one I can't do without.' I couldn't help but laugh and as we made our way back to our room I knew Brad had never had any affection in his life and I had had plenty.

I decided that if Brad wanted me for the weekend I was prepared to stay. We took a shower and got into our own beds but after a few minutes I asked him to join me in my bed. He held me like I was about to fall apart in his arms and made love to me like I was sure he had never done before. Afterwards he asked me if he should go to his own bed and I told him he only had to leave if he wanted to. He was still there with me in the morning.

I didn't realise it at the time, but being with Brad was the start of my recovery from Joe. I still felt the scars of the wretched way Joe and I had been forced to part. I never thought I would ever recover. But Brad's wicked sense of humour reminded me how to have fun and during the last few days I came to know that behind that rough exterior was a really nice guy.

I had just a few days left in Germany and Brad wanted to come back to England with me. So he applied for leave and arrived in England the day after me. We met in a Covent Garden wine bar and Brad suggested we go back to his hotel but wouldn't say where he was staying.

In the cab he asked the driver to go to the Savoy. He surely couldn't mean the real Savoy? But he did. It turned out to be a decadent weekend with Brad treating me like a prince. He even came to the train station with me and asked if he could write.

But we couldn't quite wait that long. He'd given me the phone number of the hotel he had moved into, so I called him when I got off the train. 'How would you like to spend a few days here in Cheltenham?' I asked. There was some sort of commotion at the other end of the phone, it sounded like he'd dropped it in his excitement. 'When can I come?' he asked. 'Well, I had better check it out with my parents. I'll call you back.' 'Miss you,' he whispered down the line. I called

Mother and she said it would be fine to bring Brad home to the Inn.

Suddenly it felt strange to be taking Brad home with me where we would no doubt be sleeping together. I felt a traitor to Mark even though he was to be married soon. When I thought of the nights Mark and I made love in my room it somehow didn't feel quite right to be there with anyone else. Then I thought that I must put the past behind me. My relationship with Mark was over, or so I thought.

So I phoned Brad and he took the next train. I shoved my belongings in left luggage and waited impatiently in the café for him. When he arrived he threw his arms about me and waltzed me around and around on the platform. We took a taxi and as we drove through the countryside Brad, an inner-city boy, was amazed at how beautiful it was.

There was quite a fuss when we got to the Inn, I'd been away for two years and returned with a handsome man in tow.

'You'll have to share a bed with John, I hope that's all right,' said Mother. 'Sure,' said Brad with a broad smile on his face as he looked at me. Mother, in my absence, had replaced the two single beds in my room with a large king size. I couldn't believe the renovation work that had been done to the Inn, we now had hot and cold running water and my bedroom had an en suite with shower.

Brad seemed in awe of the Inn. 'What a great place to grow up. I didn't know life could be like this.' Mother prepared a show-stopping meal and Brad had several second helpings and continually thanked my parents for their hospitality.

Father and Brad started chatting about the Service while I helped Mother with the dishes. 'How's Mark?' I asked. 'He's fine, but a little put out that he can't stay tonight. He's been practically living here since you went away. All the guest rooms are full so I couldn't put him up,' she replied.

After dinner, as I unpacked, I noticed some of Mark's clothes in the wardrobe. I felt funny just catching his scent on them.

My parents had organised a welcome home party for me and had invited Mark, his fiancée Rita and some of his football friends. Mother, of course, invited Brad to stay for the party.

Mark and Brad's meeting wasn't quite the controlled situation I'd hoped for. Mother offered Mark one of the guest rooms for the night of the party and so I was forced to introduce them when they met in the hallway. I could see how angry Mark was. Dragging me off down the corridor, Mark looked at me with fury in his eyes. 'Who is he, what is he doing here? I should be sharing with you and he should be in the guest room. How long is he staying?' Mark rattled off.

'Hold on a moment, Mark, Brad's a friend of mine. We met in the Forces as we were in the same squadron in Germany, he's had a tough life and I thought it would be good for him to see what a happy home was like. He certainly didn't have anything like it when he was growing up.'

Taking a deep breath I started again as he tried to interrupt me. 'You have no right to be angry, I didn't hear from you for ages and then I get a letter saying you're getting married. You'd obviously moved on!' I squawked.

Mark was visibly shaking at my outburst. 'You are getting married in a week so I don't know what you are moaning about,' I snapped. Stomping away I cursed Mother for inviting him to my welcome home party.

As soon as I walked into the party I spotted Mark at a table with Rita. I didn't know her very well and yet I didn't like her. I watched as his wife-to-be poured drink after drink down her neck and later, completely drunk, tripped and spilled her drink all over Mark.

I'd first seen Rita a few nights earlier when I was on a night out with Brad in Cheltenham. She was with a group of girlfriends and even from a distance we could tell she was drunk. Weaving her way over to us, she stumbled as she reached our table.

'You're John, eh, a friend of Mark? And who is this, your boyfriend?' she slurred as she held on to the edge of the table to steady herself.

'This is Brad, a friend I made in the RAF,' I replied, trying to keep my cool. 'Hello, Brad. You're a bit of all right, aren't you?' she smirked, and staggered off back to her friends. We weren't aware of the music starting at first but it soon became quite wild in the bar. Then we watched in horror as Rita leapt onto a table, wiggling around and looking as if she would lose her footing at any moment. The Stripper came on the jukebox, a loud voice from the other side of the pub shouted, 'Take 'em off, love!' and Rita responded at once. Before long she was down to her panties, then she keeled over, falling off the end of the table into the arms of two young guys.

Now for the second time, at my own party, I was watching her get completely paralytic and I wondered what Mark saw in her. The night before I asked my ever-stoical Mother whether she thought I should talk to Mark about what I'd seen.

'It really isn't any of our business, and I can't help thinking it will only cause more upset if you try to tell him about this. It's just not worth making things so unpleasant that we are not even on speaking terms with him. He's chosen to marry her and if he can't see the problems he's going to have, there's nothing we can do to stop it.'

Brad was dreading leaving and going back to Germany but was more concerned about my fight with Mark. 'You slept with him, didn't you?' he questioned gently. 'Yes, I did, before the RAF, but as you can see he's about to marry Rita and I'm with you tonight.'

The next morning I drove Brad to the train station in Father's car. Tears formed in his eyes as he tried to say goodbye, and as I watched the train leave the station and disappear out of sight I felt sad. That night I had to break the tension and so decided to meet some of the old football crew in the pub. I knew Mark would be there and decided I would tackle the awkwardness by offering him a drink. 'Fancy a pint?' I said. He grabbed his drink with a false smile and sat down in the corner of the bar, then I joined him.

'Is he gone?' Mark said. 'Brad left this morning,' I replied.

'I couldn't stand him being with you,' he said. 'Why?' I replied. 'You know very well why,' he said. 'No, I don't,' I replied. The redness in his cheeks showed how angry he was getting.

'Look, Mark, what do you want from me? I read your letter saying you were going to get married so what makes you think I would expect to start sleeping with you again?' I continued. 'What do you think I've been doing for the last two years? You're not the only guy to fancy me, I can tell you. Tell me why you can't stand Brad being with me. What do you think I'll be doing when you are married – waiting in my bed each night just in case you have the urge to sleep with me once in a while? Because if that's what you think, I can tell you, you'll be disappointed.'

My outburst seemed to calm Mark down. 'I know what you are saying makes sense but it doesn't stop me feeling jealous if I see you with someone else,' he said, so quietly I struggled to hear. 'But if your feelings are so strong then why get married?' I replied. I took his long pause as an indication he was thinking about things rather than looking for excuses. He explained he was only doing what was expected of him and what his parents wanted.

'Mark, nobody can make you marry. If you are doing it to

please your parents it's the wrong reason, though you must have said something to Rita to convince her you should take that decision,' I said. I was struggling to understand his motives. Mark seemed intent on ignoring his true feelings and making me the victim of his bad decisions. I could feel my anger festering as I carried on my frustrated attempt to keep calm. I was losing control of my temper. Mark clearly couldn't see the unhappiness he was about to inflict on both of us. I slammed my drink down on the table. 'All right, go and get married. I don't care,' I shouted loud enough for the whole bar to hear, and stormed from the room.

I knew there was no way I could just go to bed and sleep, I was too wound up and stressed after my row with Mark. I couldn't understand him wanting to live his life to please his parents. If he didn't know he was gay I certainly did. Trying to tell me it was just a bit of fun was nonsense and made my blood boil. I walked around trying to cool my temper. I was normally a placid person but this situation really got to me. I had assumed that my relationship with Mark was over two years ago and now he was more or less telling me he wanted to start all over again. I was not about to come between two people who were marrying so I decided to try and keep Mark at arm's length until the wedding day. At least, that was my intention.

I felt exhausted after all the drama of the evening and got straight into bed when I got home. I went into a deep sleep but around two in the morning I woke up to hear knocking on my French doors. I knew instantly it was Mark and leapt out of the bed to open the door. He just grabbed me and it was as if the last two years had never existed. He didn't say a word as he laid me back on the bed, and he really didn't have to.

I woke in the morning as Mother put the tea tray down on the side table. Mark's arms were holding on to me as if I might try to escape. He was firm asleep. Mother smiled, winked at me and closed the door.

That afternoon Mother told me she had invited Mark to dinner. 'You know Mark is like another son we never had. We've become very fond of him, and he spent almost all his time here when you were away – he did bar work for us so that we could take time off and he wouldn't accept any payment. But I am worried about you: what is going to happen when he gets married?' Mother asked.

'Don't ask me, Mother, I have no idea, but I have told him our relationship has to end when that happens,' I replied.

'She's so wrong for him, I can't stand her. Why he ever got involved I'll never know,' said Mother. 'I've told him to come to dinner tonight then maybe you can have a talk with him.'

'Mother, I've said all I have to say on the subject. If he wants to get married to please his parents there is nothing I can do about it.'

Dinner that evening was not pleasant, there was a tension that had never existed before and we were all keen to get out and have a walk in the fresh air.

So Mark and I went up to the highest point of the hill behind the Inn, which had a view over the river Severn in the distance. 'When you look down from here it makes all your problems seem very small,' I said. I'm sorry, I just couldn't find any words to say at dinner,' he said. 'I guess the two years away sorted out your feelings. You know you're gay, that's something, whereas I seem to be in an impossible muddle,' he said sadly.

'Don't you consider yourself gay after last night?' I said. 'My folks would kill me if I admitted that,' replied Mark.

'So you're going to live a lie just to please your parents? That's crazy – and where does it leave us?'

Mark asked if he could stay with me until the wedding. I had no idea what Mother or Father would make of it, although I was sure by now they knew what was going on. When we got back to the Inn Mark went for a shower so I sat Mother down. 'Is the tiff over, does he still love you?'

I didn't know quite where to start. I know it looked bad that Brad had just left and now I was back in the arms of Mark. I told her Mark wanted to stay until the wedding.

'Mark knows he is welcome to stay any time whether you are friends or not, but if you are, what I want to know is will he be sleeping one night with her and the next with you?' said Mother. 'Mother, I've told you before it will stop after the wedding,' I said, not quite believing my own words.

Mark walked in on the end of our conversation. 'I know you both think I'm mad but I have to give it a try, it's too late to back out now,' he said. 'Mark, you're not trying on a new pair of shoes, this is supposed to be for life. I know you and John have been sleeping together for years, let's not pretend otherwise,' she said. Feeling embarrassed, Mark made his excuses and exit while Mother sat with me and I explained how Mark had found himself in this situation.

As soon as I'd gone off to Germany, Mark had set about finding himself a girlfriend – his parents were keen to marry him off to any girl that would have him. Clare, who he had been seeing before I left, decided she preferred a rugby player so Mark started going regularly to all the dances. Rita turned out to be his next date after Clare. In the beginning she was the perfect girlfriend and Mark really thought he had found the one. The only thing that unnerved him was Rita's parents, an odd couple who visited the kind of clubs you don't talk about in polite company. However, Rita seemed demure and conservative and he soon introduced her to his parents. She became a regular visitor, spending most nights with Mark to avoid the problems at home.

My parents liked Rita too, at least at first. But after a few visits to the Inn Mother began to think that Rita was not at all what she seemed. Mother couldn't quite decide why she didn't like her but she didn't say a word to Mark. Each time she turned up at the Inn with Mark she became more relaxed and even Father noticed she might not turn out to be the virginal bride that she portrayed herself as.

One night Rita came into the bar without Mark, he was

still at a football match. Mother was surprised that she decided to come into the bar alone as it wasn't the kind of thing you would expect a girl of her age to do. She ordered a glass of wine and then another.

By the time Mark arrived she was on her fourth or fifth, Mother had lost count. She begun to slur her words and Mark became increasingly annoyed, eventually dragging her out the door as she protested. He thought it would be an isolated incident; after all, she'd never behaved like that before and probably never would again.

A few weeks later Mark took Rita out. After a lovely meal they ended up on the settee in Rita's house. Rita went upstairs for a few minutes and returned with nothing on but her panties. Pouncing on Mark, she tried to take his trousers off, reaching his ankles just as Rita's parents walked in. Mark hurriedly pulled up his trousers and without a word made for the door. Rita's parents weren't keen to let go of what they'd seen and demanded an explanation. Rita decided to tell them Mark had proposed.

And so the wedding train set off before Mark could stop it. Rita's mother sent out wedding invitations, before long wedding gifts began to arrive. Mark knew nothing of this until people began congratulating him and he knew he was trapped. Rita even threatened to sue Mark if he didn't go through with it and his parents were over the moon, finally free of the burden of their final child. This was when I got the letter asking me to be best man.

The marriage

In the days before the wedding Mark spent all his time with me and barely saw Rita. It was our last fling before he started living his lie.

Two days before the wedding I was clearing up the kitchen when Father appeared. 'Am I too late for coffee?' Father asked. 'Just sit there in your usual place and I'll get some for you,' I replied. Father never said much to me. He never wasted words, you knew when he spoke he would say something meaningful. 'I'm worried about you, are you going to be all right after this marriage'? Father asked. ' Father, don't worry about me. I've learnt a lot in the last couple of years. I know there is more out there, even if I'm about to lose someone really important – you know, plenty more fish in the sea,' I replied. He laughed and said, 'Anybody who hooks up with you will land an even more important one.'

The wedding ceremony was simple and faultless. By the time we reached the reception Rita had had more than a few cocktails and flew straight into insulting Mark's aunt and smashing the top layer of the wedding cake on her head. Mark bolted across the room to restrain her and slipped over, ending up under a table, while Mark's aunt took her revenge by hurling a glass of red wine over the bride. Several of the guests, including Mark's parents, decided it was time to leave. The rest stayed around to see how bad things would get.

Rita was sobbing uncontrollably and I took her to a room

to change clothes while Mark ordered a taxi. Rita returned with her hair falling all over her face and her hat at a very strange angle. She looked like she'd arrived from an all-night party. They sped off in the taxi and I went back into the hall to pour myself a stiff drink. I hadn't seen my parents during the reception but caught sight of them on the other side of the hall. Mother was wearing the most hideous hat I had ever seen and I was sure it was in protest. 'Where did you get that terrible hat?' I asked. 'I know, it was the worst one I could find,' she replied. 'What a disaster this wedding is, I've never been to one like it,' she said, with a wicked smile on her face. 'Poor Mark, he's in for an awful time.'

I spent the next few days relaxing alone. Occasionally I'd think of Mark and Rita on their honeymoon and I genuinely hoped the good weather and surroundings would settle them both. I had to sign up at college for the final part of my interior design course and it brought back sad memories: I'd dreamt Mark and I would open a business together, a dream I knew was now gone. I was quite down and decided a few drinks with Mark's mates would cheer me up. I rolled home late after a few drinks and fell asleep immediately. I woke up to a familiar tapping noise. Mark stood, soaked to the skin, outside the French doors. 'What the hell are you doing here?' I asked. 'Just let me get out of these wet things, for God's sake make me a hot toddy, and I'll tell you,' he replied, shivering.

He then told me Rita had continued drinking on the way to their honeymoon, caused a row at the check-in desk, dropped her bag off and went straight to the bar, where she stayed for several hours. When she'd finally come to bed she passed out, fully clothed, and snored all night long. Mark had spent the next day alone on the beach, knowing he'd made a horrible mistake. That afternoon he called, booked a flight home and left a note saying he couldn't stand it any longer. We sat in silence drinking our hot toddy. 'I haven't slept for three nights so I'm really tired. Do you mind if we don't talk any more and just go to sleep?' Mark said. 'That's all right by me,' I replied. So we switched off the light and both fell into a deep sleep.

Mother arrived on cue in the morning. She banged the tray down on the table to wake us. 'I don't know why you're here but I'm not surprised,' she said. At breakfast Father got up from the table and reached for Mark's hand. 'We are so glad to see you, Mark. You don't have to tell us why you came back so soon. We're just happy you came back to us.' I was astonished. Father never made extravagant gestures but it was obvious he thought a lot of Mark. 'You may not want the gory details, but I do,' said Mother.

Mark took his time. 'I hope you didn't mind me staying last night but there was no way I could face the family. I know they will think it's my fault that the marriage didn't work out.' 'You can stay as long as you like,' said Father.

'So I guess the marriage is off, but she wasn't the right girl for you,' said Father. 'I found that out the hard way,' replied Mark. 'I never actually asked her to marry me, before I knew it she and her mother had organised everything. And I never consummated the marriage, so I am going to get an annulment'. 'You're well out of it,' consoled Mother. 'Now I've got a week and a half's holiday left and nowhere to go,' said Mark. 'I'll come with you if you feel like going somewhere,' I said. 'Why don't you go down to the Haven Hotel at Sandbanks Peninsular?' said Father. 'It's a wonderful place if you get the weather.' Mother offered to book us a room.

We set out in Mark's new sports car with the hood down and drove non-stop to the hotel. We arrived at a grand-looking hotel around lunchtime, and blue skies greeted us. I was too worried about money to take in the view but it turned out my parents had paid for the first week and Mark had money left over from his fated honeymoon. When I got to the check-in desk the male clerk gave me a funny look. 'Top floor, room 101,' he said. The room was truly amazing, a suite complete with wedding card and champagne. Roaring with laughter we realised mother must have mentioned a honeymoon and they were expecting newlyweds. 'Shall we tell them?' I said. 'No, let's have some fun. There may be some more free drinks to come,' replied Mark. We spent the afternoon exploring the local beaches, taking the chain ferry to Shell Bay and discovering a nudist area where we swam naked in the sea.

We decided to have dinner at the hotel that evening, so in our best suits and ties we were ushered, by the head waiter, to a table near the window where we could see the boats sailing into the harbour. Nearby there were two ladies on separate tables eating alone. After a while one of them turned to us and asked if we were on holiday. I replied that we were. She was obviously a lady of means, wearing the fabulous clothes and a very expensive-looking diamond brooch. The rest of the diners turned to watch as she spoke, her expensively-dyed blonde hair twinkling in the evening light of the room.

Mark suddenly said, 'John and I are on our honeymoon.' I kicked Mark under the table. 'Oh, how existentialist,' she said with a smile.

The lady on the next table, who was pouring wine, was so shocked at what she heard that she overfilled the glass and it ran across the tablecloth. A waiter hastily arrived to mop up and change the cloth. The fuss allowed me to have a good look at our other dinner companion who also seemed to be well-off. Like Ursula she was probably in her sixties but perfectly turned out, with silver-grey hair – one of the most elegant women I'd ever seen.

The first lady continued, peering at us with penetrating green eyes, 'I'm Ursula Peterson. I live in Stratford-upon-Avon and I'm absolutely fascinated by your frankness. Of course it doesn't shock me – you see, I have been in the theatre most of my life. When I was in my prime I was in many musical shows. My first husband was in diamonds import/export and he was practically eaten by a lion when on safari. My second husband was a banker, terribly tedious; he expired while in bed with another young actress. I believe there was a terrible uproar at the time as he was handcuffed to the bed, horrible job cutting him free.'

Our wine-spilling lady friend, Margery, then decided to fill us in on her life. 'I've had some experiences, too: I had to marry into money at an early age as father had lost everything on the stock exchange. My husband knew I didn't love him and went out to find someone who did. He was very generous and gave me lots of money that would allow me to live in a grand way for the rest of my life. So I helped my family first and then went on a world cruise where I met the love of my life, Sir Stanley Hadley. After a while I found that he was broke and was stealing large amounts of my money. Fortunately I had most of my wealth in a Swiss bank account so I disappeared one day and I have never seen him since.'

Mark asked if she'd ever married again. 'No dear, it's far too much trouble. I just took a lover.' All this and we hadn't even got to the main course. It looked like we were in for an interesting week with Ursula and Margery.

Mark was keen to keep up the pretence that we were on honeymoon but I didn't think it was right to keep our new lady friends in the dark. So the next morning I spotted them both at breakfast and explained our situation.

'But you are together?' asked Ursula. I didn't know quite how to reply, given the events of the last few weeks. 'Well, I guess we are. I'm not quite sure what that means – Mark has been married and practically divorced in the last few weeks,' I replied. 'It all sounds terribly complicated,' said Margery. 'Do you sleep together?' Ursula whispered so that no one could hear. 'Sometimes,' I replied. 'We are a couple on this holiday and have been, in one way or another, since we were seventeen.' Margery seemed unfazed. 'In my book you look perfectly suited and I can't think why you wanted to get married, it's a recipe for disaster,' she said.

On our final night we plumped for a farewell dinner with our ladies. We were all in high spirits, drinking far too much wine and then our usual brandy and coffee.

'It's been a pleasure meeting you boys, and I hope we will meet again very soon,' said Ursula. 'Now, you both get your lives sorted out. Time is very short: you may not think so at your age, but believe me, before you know it life has passed you by,' said Margery. The ladies retired for the evening and I watched Mark staring out across the moonlit sea, desperately holding in something he obviously needed to say.

'I've been thinking about what the ladies said to us about living our lives in limbo. I know I used to say to you not to take what was happening to us too seriously and that it was just a bit of fun, but I think I was taking this attitude as a defence from the reality of the situation, an escape,' he said.

'Since you've been back and during this holiday, it's clear to me what I want and that's life with you. Do you feel the same way or am I making a complete fool of myself?' he asked.

'You must know by now that my feelings have been the same as yours, I've just been waiting for you to decide if you can make the commitment,' I replied. Mark took his signet ring off his finger and put it on mine. 'We're the real deal, then,' he said.

Mark then asked me what my plans were for when we went home. He told me about a cottage in the country not far from Cheltenham that his uncle had left to him. 'It's in need of a total renovation. We could work on it and then move in together,' he explained. I instantly loved the idea but was worried about what our parents and the football lads would think.

'As long as you're there I couldn't care less about what anyone else thinks,' said Mark. 'My family have no idea my uncle left me the cottage as he had no contact with them for years. As for my friends, anyone who wants to cut loose can. It will show they were not a true friend in the first place,' he continued. My reservations melted away and I was desperate to see the cottage as soon as we got back.

The next morning we reluctantly left the Haven and drove back to the Inn to share our plans with my parents. 'We've got something to tell you,' I said, looking directly at my parents across the scarred oak kitchen table, scared of the words that were about to come out of my mouth. I told them all about the cottage in the country. My father, ever practical, wanted to know exactly what would happen once we moved in together.

'If he helps me get the place in shape I will make him co-owner,' said Mark. 'That's very generous, but from what you say it's going to take serious money for the renovations. If

Mother and I help you with the finance, then we would be happy for you to make John co-owner,' said Father. We decided to take a family trip down to the cottage. It was a pretty house with a thatched roof, down a private lane and well away from other properties. The garden was a jungle, but it was a large plot that had endless possibilities and a cute summerhouse at the end.

We opened the front door to a large lounge with a huge fireplace and chocked full of old furniture. The kitchen had a cooker and nothing much else, the bathroom was the same sorry story. The bedroom was not particularly large, with an old bedstead and views across the rolling Cotswold hills.

'Mark, you're the architect – how much do you think it's going to take to put this cottage in order?' asked Father. 'It could be done for about fifteen thousand, maybe less,' Mark replied. 'Mother and I will put in twenty thousand, which will give you some extra to furnish. We had better tie things up legally and then John can become co-owner.' Mother hugged Mark and Father shook his hand, and our new life began.

As I saw my parents to their car my father had one final question. 'I'm concerned about the size of the bedroom. Is it big enough to get two single beds in there?' said Father. Mark looked up from his notes and smiled at me. I was about to say something but Mark signalled not to. After all, we had the rest of our lives to explain.

Renovations started between my college work and Mark's job. We employed tradesman to do the technical jobs but soon moved in so we could help out. We took our first shopping trip as a couple, accompanied by Mother who was sure we had no idea how to shop.

'We had better go to the bed department first. You've got to have somewhere to sleep,' Mother said. When we got there she went straight to the singles. We headed off to the king sizes.

'This is why I didn't want her to come,' I whispered to Mark. 'Let's take her for a coffee. We are going to have to tell her,' said Mark. So we glanced at the single beds to pacify her and took her to the café. After we had finished our coffee I decided to just go for it. 'Mother, it's a little embarrassing but we are not interested in single beds. We're only interested in a king size.' 'But won't you be sort of on top of one another?' Mark and I just fell about laughing.

'What are you laughing about?' she said. Every time we started to explain we just started off again until she started laughing. 'Oh, you want to sleep together,' she replied. 'Yes, Mother, we certainly do. You see, Mark and I have been an item for quite some time. We can't wait to live together.' She said, 'You know, I said to your father some time ago that I thought you were having some sort of affair but he wouldn't believe it. He thought Mark couldn't possibly be gay as he plays football and mends his car.' That started us off laughing again. She said she would explain to Father the situation to avoid any further confusion. She said she didn't think Father would mind about us being together as long as Mark mended his car.

The cottage

That Friday we moved into the cottage and invited my parents for Sunday lunch.

Father seemed a little embarrassed at first but relaxed after a good lunch and the best part of a bottle of wine. 'I must say that you boys have done a great job on the cottage. Of course, I haven't seen the upstairs since you finished it,' said Father.

Mark took him upstairs. I heard Father's comments floating down. 'You got over the problem of fitting two singles in here, then,' said Father; I could hear the grin. Mark couldn't help smiling back. 'You know, if I didn't have Mother, I'd fancy a setup like this.'

We had my parents' approval but some friends and family were shocked we'd moved in together. It wasn't widely accepted that two men would live together, although little did we know that in our own lifetime our kind of relationship would become commonplace and acceptable. But our critics were in the minority and we paid them little attention. Then one night Mark was walking home from football practice when two guys appeared from nowhere and beat him up so badly he ended up in hospital. Mark's two friends, Peter and Steven, found him unconscious, lying on a footpath close to the practice ground. I had the feeling something like this would happen, there were always fanatical gay-bashers ready to inflict harm if they had the opportunity. I raced to the hospital when I got the call. I walked into his room but he was hardly visible for bandages, all I could see were his two black eyes. He was awake. 'It's probably a silly question, but how do you feel?' I asked. 'Not so good,' Mark whispered. He pulled his hand out from underneath the covers and put it in mine. 'Do you regret us moving in together after this?' I asked. 'Don't even go there. I'd do it again tomorrow: I don't care what others think, my life is with you. You must know that by now,' he replied. 'Do you know who it was that did this to you?' I asked. 'Yes, it wasn't as if they had masks on, they wanted me to know who they were. It was two new lads in the team,' Mark replied drowsily. I stayed there with him, falling asleep in the chair beside the bed. No one asked me to leave and I woke up there the next morning.

Mark was in hospital several days for observation but he was a strong lad and soon began to recover. Peter, Steven and I took it in shifts to be with him and we all went to collect him when he was discharged. Mark didn't want the police involved so the two lads thought they'd got away with it. The club had other ideas. No one in the team would speak to them and they eventually left the club, and us, alone.

I was worried that this was an indication of things to come and decided to phone Margery and Ursula to let them know what had happened and for advice. They wanted to come and see us but I told them Mark was on the mend. Margery insisted that she hold a fancy dress party in Mark's honour, as soon as he was well enough. I told her I wanted to bring Peter and Steven as they'd been so good to Mark, although I did wonder how two straight married men would fit in with the gay, theatre crowd. When I asked them, their reaction wasn't quite what I expected: 'Just try to stop us coming. We're already making costumes for the party.'

A few days after Mark came out of hospital we were lounging on the settee, his feet in my lap as we watched a film on television. There was a loud hammering on the front door. I got up to open it and Mark's father almost pushed me over as he entered, closely followed by Mark's mother. I asked them both to sit but they stayed standing, in their coats.

'To what do we owe this pleasure?' asked Mark. His father's face was full of rage. 'Why weren't we told you were in hospital?' spat his father. 'I wasn't in any danger. It was mainly for observation,' replied Mark. 'I think you deserved all you got and more for the disgraceful way you are living with him.' By now his father was yelling and pointing at me.

'How you can pass up a perfectly good marriage to spend your life living like this I don't know,' his father finished. Mark had now stood up to face his father. 'That perfectly good marriage was to a woman who was a raging alcoholic and I felt nothing for Rita, I was mad to even consider marrying her. There is only one person in my life and that's John, I just wish I had realised it sooner.'

'How can you sit there and say such a thing, bringing disgrace on the family? What do you think your brothers will think when they find out?' said his mother. 'I would hope they would understand and wish me luck,' replied Mark.

'Well, I'm telling you now I will not allow this to continue. Get this guy out of here,' he said pointing to me. Mark went white with anger. 'John is not going anywhere and our lives are none of your business, we are consenting adults behind closed doors. We never flaunt our situation in front of others or interfere with anyone: our lives are private and if you and Mother can't accept that, I think it better if you never visit us again.'

'So you put him before our family?' said his father. 'He is my family and this is our home and I suggest you leave it now, before any more hurtful things are said,' replied Mark. 'Throwing your own mother and father out of your house after all we have done for you, that's very nice, I must say. And you, corrupting our son like this, it's a crime. I should report you to the police,' said Mark's father. 'If there was any corrupting being done it was me long ago, not John. I refused to accept what I truly felt for years and the only time I've been happy in my adult life is being with John and that is the truth of the matter. So as I have told you, if you still think it better for outward appearances' sake to live an unhappy miserable life married in my situation, we have nothing left to say to one another.'

They almost ran out the door. I could see Mark's mother didn't agree with everything his father had said, but was too frightened to say anything. I went across to the drinks cabinet and poured both of us a large brandy. 'I feel terrible alienating you from your family,' I said to Mark. 'You are not the cause. I realise I would have chosen this way of life anyway, even if we had never met. After all, it was me who started hitting on you, not the other way around. I just hope I didn't send you in the wrong direction all that time ago,' said Mark. 'Even if you hadn't started something with me, I knew when I was in the RAF that my true orientation was in this direction and you weren't even around at the time,' I replied. We lay on the settee, happy in each other's arms, until it was time for bed.

The following evening we were sitting on the settee again, trying to watch another film. There was another knock on our door. I opened it to find my parents on the doorstep. 'We've just come to see how Mark is,' said Mother. I let them in and she walked across to the settee and kissed Mark on the forehead. 'How are you feeling, Mark?' she said. 'Not so bad, I'll be back to normal in a few days.' 'I hope we're not intruding,' said Father. 'No, it's fine, we were only watching television. We had a visit from Mark's parents last night, we haven't quite got over it yet,' I replied. Mark smiled and said, 'They think we're immoral and that I deserved all I got from those thugs. I made it quite clear to them that we didn't care what they thought and we would be living together regardless of what anyone did or said. I don't think we will be seeing them again. Anyway, I've regarded you both as my second parents and as long as we have your support, nothing matters.' 'You know you can always call on us at any time,' said Mother. Father shook Mark's hand and gave him a hug. 'Will you have a drink with us?' I asked. 'That would be nice,' said Father. We sat chatting for a while and then my parents left.

'What a difference to my parents,' said Mark. 'Yes, but you know your parents just don't understand our lifestyle and we really can't expect them to. They might come around, you know, Mark – after all, they do love you,' I replied, as I stared into the sadness apparent in his eyes. But even as I said it I didn't quite believe it. I wasn't sure if I even cared. They treated me as second rate: the fact that I wasn't a woman and able to bear children was clearly too much for them to handle. I stared down at my hands, the blood slowly returning to my knuckles where they'd been clenched against the hatred spewing from his parents. The only thing that had stopped me pushing his father's beetroot face out of the door was keeping Mark's relationship with them intact – after all, they were his parents.

Mark's parents weren't overflowing with love, they were cold people and had systematically pushed away their children and grandchildren. I inwardly laughed at the idea of us producing even more offspring that they could ignore and thought it a good job it wasn't biologically possible. Mark was curled up in one of our corduroy armchairs, the ice cubes in his whisky disappearing in the flames of the open fire.

'I'm just glad we have your parents,' he said, as he lifted his glass to his lips. I turned away from the fire, tears filling my eyes as I remembered all the times my parents had a gentle smile and a nice word for Mark. Probably more love and attention than he'd ever had from his own kin. I thought back to the first time Mother found us in bed together: instead of judgement and anger, Mark found a humorous wink and warmth. Mark would always have a place in our family.

'At least we have the support of my parents. We could have had no contact with our families at all. Can you imagine what some couples in our position face? Never seeing or speaking to either set of parents?' I said. Mark was lost in his own thoughts. He couldn't help regretting the prospect of no contact with his parents, brothers or nieces and nephews.

'I guess they have a warped idea of gayness, I know some people think it's perverted or wrong. Maybe your parents think they can catch being gay!' I half-joked, hoping to bring some light to the conversation. 'I think I have to leave it up to my family to approach me, when they are ready,' Mark said. Despite Mark's hope I knew in my heart that his family were unlikely to ever want to be part of our lives. We'd already discussed spending Christmas alone at the cottage, a change from his usual festive celebrations with family. His parents were so set in their ways and if they were unwilling to embrace me as part of their family then Mark didn't want to spend time with them.

I wished there was some way to make Mark's parents see how unbelievably happy we were living together. Maybe if they knew how much we loved each other perhaps they could learn to forgive us. I wanted the whole world to know how we felt. I wanted everyone to share in our happiness.

As we lay in bed that night I watched Mark's calm,

sleeping face. I wanted a happy and full life with him. I couldn't imagine him not being part of my life. I wondered if I'd missed out on happiness by spending time in the RAF when I could have been with Mark, but I didn't regret my time with Joe and knew he'd taught me how to really love.

We'd resigned ourselves to a quiet Christmas at home and on Christmas Eve we stoked the open fire and exchanged gifts. There was a knock at the door and, not expecting any visitors, Mark looked at me quizzically.

Mark's brother, Simon, was standing there, loaded up with parcels. I offered Simon a drink and he seemed a nice guy but I was wondering what he thought about me and our situation. It wasn't long before I found out.

He told us he'd been working away and didn't have our telephone number or he would have called a long time before. He seemed quite unfazed by Mark and me living together. A few glasses of wine eased us into difficult conversation territory. 'I always knew Mark was gay and was completely confused when he got married. I'm pleased for him that he came to his senses and got you to live with him,' he said.

He went on to explain. 'It's a relief to know he's settled with someone nice. My other brother will have nothing to do with Mark. He is just like our parents, totally intolerant. I'm different: live and let live, I say. Mark has no idea but some years ago I had a relationship with a male friend of mine – his parents moved away and he went with them – so how can I stand in judgement of your relationship?' he finished, to looks of shock from both me and Mark.

'I then met my wife and my life changed. We are very happy and have two great kids, it's a change around but probably for the better. I wouldn't want all the hassle you two are going through,' he continued.

'It's great to know someone in his family doesn't consider him to be an outcast,' I replied. Simon soon made his excuses, he had to get back to his young family, but he left us with an invitation to come to their house the next day.

I could see by Mark's face it had made his Christmas to see his brother and have the invite. Christmas Day turned out not to be quite the dour affair we'd imagined: we spent the day with Simon, his lovely wife and their chaotic and noisy kids. I watched with pride as Mark threw himself back into his family life, a place he belonged.

The day of Margery's party arrived and the four of us made our way to London in my car. Ursula was dressed as Queen Victoria in a fabulous costume she had borrowed from the Royal Shakespeare Company. Peter and Steven were dressed as the two ugly sisters. Mark and I had on Roman costumes. Rupert, a friend of Margery's, and his friend arrived as Dracula and a witch. Margery had hired caterers who brought in plate after plate of wonderful food and a flaming punch bowl. Margery, dressed as Goldilocks, served the punch and as usual played the piano and sang. Peter and Steven seemed quite at home and I wondered if their marriages were as happy as they made out.

Mark had become quite a theatre buff and wanted to see all the new shows in London. Rupert was very kind and got us wonderful seats for most of the shows and we'd stay at Margery's house each time we went to the city. She'd often come with us to see a new show, and sometimes Rupert would tag along, especially to the shows in small theatres that were more of a risqué nature and totally unsuitable for Margery. I told him on many occasions that she was very broadminded and I didn't think anything would shock her, but he didn't want to take the chance. After the show he took us to all sorts of clubs that, unless you lived in the city, would have no idea they existed. They were not all gay clubs, although the ones that were turned out to be totally outrageous.

It was an exciting time to be gay, people were becoming far more open about 'coming out' in the late Sixties and early Seventies. I loved people-watching, gawping at the mad outfits and the courage those men had to wear them. It was fun, but there was always an undercurrent of tension.

Gay men were mugged and even killed in bad areas at night and there were police raids on well known gay places. Men were arrested and charged for hardly any reason at all. One night Rupert took us to a notorious gay club in the East End. There was a funny cabaret with glamorous performers that looked like celebrities.

Halfway through the performance the police arrived, loaded us all into vans and took us down to the police station. Fortunately Mark and I weren't charged but we became less relaxed about the clubs we went to. Rupert did tell us that he'd seen several of the policemen from that night back in the clubs when they were off duty, obviously intrigued by what they had seen.

After Mark and I had been living together for a year we decided we could no longer hide the truth from his parents. Their questions, designed to get at what was going on, were becoming ever more ludicrous. Mark was bored of making up stories, so we invited both sets of parents to a barbeque one day in the summer.

The afternoon started pleasantly, our parents chatting despite not knowing each other very well. Mark's parents had been told that Mark had inherited the cottage and constantly referred to it as 'Mark's house'. Every time they said this phrase I could see my father squirming in his seat.

The final crunch came when Mark's father referred to me as Mark's lodger. 'John is not Mark's lodger, he has worked hard on the cottage to get it into its present condition and that we are close friends sharing the accommodation,' snapped Father.

It put Mark's parents in their place without letting Mark down by revealing the true relationship. All the while Mark was silent, I said we would be serving the food and everyone was to get themselves a drink from the bar. When nobody was looking I glanced across at Mark and we smiled at one another. It seemed ridiculous that we had to go through this charade.

There was one scary moment when his mother started wandering up the stairs, looking for the bathroom. Mark managed to steer her in the right direction, just as she was opening the bedroom door. Just before they left Mark's mother said, 'We'll have to do another barbeque at our house soon.' Mark looked at me and raised his eyebrows. The thought of us going through this ordeal again was more than either of us could take.

After everyone had gone home Mark and I collapsed on the settee exhausted. Mark said, 'I never want to do anything like this again, it's too stressful.' 'I couldn't agree with you more,' I replied. Mark said, 'Isn't it strange, I'm perfectly at ease with your parents, but totally on edge with mine. Can you imagine what it would have been like if both sets of parents were like mine?' We laughed, with some relief, at the thought.

Mark and I always seemed to think the same way about almost everything. We never argued about things, or ever seemed to be in a bad mood. The only time we had fallen out was when I brought Brad home. When we were alone together it was all peace and tranquillity. It was a good thing that we both had our own interests: Mark would go to football and I would play tennis and we could happily spend time apart or together.

We had a call from Ursula one evening inviting us to visit

her in her stunning Stratford home. It was quite large with five bedrooms, reception rooms, four bathrooms, and an enormous kitchen. The garden was quite magnificent. As we arrived she appeared in a colourful silk kimono and oriental slippers. 'Darlings,' she called out, 'it's wonderful to see you.' She threw her arms about us, kissing us on both cheeks. 'Come and see my little pad.'

As we entered everything seemed totally over the top, red walls and white carpets and huge flower arrangements all over the house. Some of the statues must have cost a fortune. The whole house was decorated in a very theatrical way. 'Now, what I've planned is a visit to the theatre and a sumptuous meal after in a really top restaurant that I know.' 'It all sounds fabulous,' I remarked. With that she closed the door and winked at us. 'Don't be too long coming down – leave the 'hanky-panky' till later!'

Mark and I felt like we had been hit by a hurricane. We just flopped down on the bed. After a while we went down to the lounge. Margery leapt up from the sofa and almost ran across the room to hug us both. 'I hope that I've not been too presumptuous putting you in the same bed. You are still an item, aren't you?' There was a silence from both of us. 'I'm so sorry,' said Ursula. 'What am I thinking of? It's only the excitement of seeing you both, I can't wait to hear your news.'

'Now, what's been going on since we were at the Haven Hotel in Sandbanks?' said Ursula. Mark said, to my amazement, 'In a nutshell, we are living together.' Both ladies let out a shriek. 'Well done,' said Margery. 'After what you said to us about life having a habit of slipping by, I think I came to my senses. I asked John if he would like to live with me and to hell with the consequences. I even gave him my signet ring to close the deal.'

'It sounds almost like a business transaction,' said Margery. 'In a way it was, as we went into a partnership on a cottage I owned, and I suppose after years of denial I realised that John and I were meant to be together, especially after my stupid attempt at marriage.' The two ladies were beside themselves.

When we arrived at the restaurant Ursula ordered a bottle of champagne and Margery was dabbing away a tear. 'It's so romantic,' she gasped. 'We also have some news: Margery has met a man! He's very rich and quite handsome,' said Ursula. 'What he sees in me I really don't know,' said Margery. 'He probably knows quality when he sees it,' I said.

Ursula said that she told Margery to be cautious after previous disasters. 'Wear a chastity belt until the ring is on her finger, I told her,' said Ursula. Margery said that sex wasn't the first thing on her mind at her age. Ursula said that it was never too late for romance. We had a wonderful evening.

They were like the two aunts we never had. Nothing we could do would be wrong in their eyes. There was a rare affection between us. Margery invited us to her house in London the next week and told us she'd booked for us all to see South Pacific at Drury Lane.

As we drove home Mark said that we were so fortunate to

have met the two ladies. It was such a change of direction for a football fanatic to appreciate the theatre and classy company, and it made me love him all the more.

Our next London trip was sensational. Apart from going to see Mary Martin in South Pacific, we were introduced to Margery's beau Cecil. He was handsome, and he obviously had money. He took us to dinner at the Savoy and tea at the Ritz. When we were invited to his yacht I imagined a small sailing boat, but when we arrived at the harbour it turned out to be a huge ocean-going craft worth thousands, complete with cocktail bar and two cabins. Cecil told us he wanted to take Margery to the Bahamas for the winter. Ursula suggested we all go and, despite Mark protesting we had to work, Ursula insisted on paying for us and flying us out.

We'd thought that Margery would be relieved to have some friends along on her first holiday with Cecil. We landed in a minor hurricane, the plane terrifyingly touching down several times before landing. We had a message from Margery saying where they were and that they had booked us into a very swish hotel where they were to meet us that evening. Margery and Cecil arrived at our dinner in paradise, Margery fussing about the hurricane and worrying about the mooring of their yacht. She seemed rather preoccupied so during a quite moment I took her to one side.

I asked her what was wrong. 'To be quite honest, John, I'm not sure I can cope with Cecil. He's very sweet and gentle but he chases me around all the time. I think he's on something, he's sexually insatiable.' I replied that it was better to have too much than too little. 'Maybe I should slap him one with the rolling pin?' 'Perhaps Ursula can help out. She's always willing to assist in a busy period,' I suggested. We couldn't stop laughing. Mark suddenly appeared and asked what was so funny. 'Margery has a hard problem,' I said. This started us off again. I told Mark later what the problem was and he suggested we tie a lead weight on the end. We had a spectacular holiday and a real insight into how the other half lived. Ursula got to know about Margery's problem but all she could say was that it wasn't a big one, as she had, quite by accident, seen Cecil in the nude. Of course, we never believed her. I didn't know this would be the last time I would be truly happy for years.

An end

One night a few weeks after our return Mark didn't come home. I called my parents to see if he had crashed out in my old room at the Inn but they hadn't seen him. There was no sign of him. I telephoned Ian, a friend of his from football, but he hadn't seen him either. I called the local police but they wouldn't tell me anything, so I called the hospital. They asked if I was a relative and when I said no they told me they couldn't tell me anything. I explained we lived together and they told me to go straight to Accident and Emergency.

I rushed down to the hospital and as I reached the

reception Mark's mother was coming out in floods of tears. 'Has Mark been in an accident?' I asked. She turned to me. 'Mark's dead,' she wailed. I felt like I was going to pass out. 'How did it happen?' I asked. 'The receptionist said it was a hit-and-run.'

I wanted to see him but I was told it wasn't a good idea so I had no alternative but to go home, feeling a loneliness I had never felt in my life. I rang my parents to tell them but I just wanted to be alone. The next few days were the saddest, darkest days of my life, wandering room to room, crying and lost in my own grief. I had to call Ursula and Margery who said they would come down for the funeral. They arrived at the cottage the night before the funeral and we spent time with my parents talking about Mark and the happier times we'd had.

The morning of the funeral I received a letter from Mark's parents' solicitor giving me notice to vacate the cottage; they were under the impression that they had inherited it from Mark. I was beside myself with anger, as if the funeral wasn't enough to bear, that they should be so grabbing to do such a thing on that day. I called Father: he was speechless with fury, and it took a lot for him to get fired up about anything. He said that I was to leave it to him.

He got on to the solicitor the same day who drew up the agreement that made me co-owner. There was a clause in the document that said that if anything happened to either of us, the surviving partner would inherit the other half. Both Mark and I had signed the agreement. Father later called me to say that there was no doubt at all that I owned the cottage. I couldn't even look at Mark's parents during the funeral.

Before the coffin was lowered into the grave, I stepped forward and placed the cross and chain he gave me before I went into the RAF on the top of his coffin and said a silent prayer. I never saw Mark's parents again.

The next year is hard to recall, it just seems blank. I became a recluse and didn't get involved with anyone romantically. I was content to be alone with myself and my memories. At one point I had counselling but it did no good, I felt as though there was no point in carrying on. I took a short holiday to the coast. Then one night when I was at my lowest ebb, I climbed onto some rocks and looked down at the dark water and wanted to end it all at that moment. Then I thought about my parents and how devastating my death would be for them. So I climbed back across the rocks, tears streaming down my face, and went into a bar and got totally plastered. While my friends partied their way through the sexual revolution and many partners, I wanted no part of it.

Nothing in my life felt the same without Mark. I would curl up in bed with his jacket, still faint with his scent on it. I could almost imagine him in the room, holding me and whispering daft jokes in my ear. The raw truth of losing him stabbed me every time the sun rose.

I put photographs of him all over the cottage. I didn't want his image to fade. His was the colour in my life and in some ways it was easier to imagine he was still with me. I refused to visit his grave and struggled to face up to the fact he was gone.

I worried that everyone was talking about me behind my back, saying how sorry they felt for me. I had constant phone calls from Ursula, Margery, Peter and Steven, desperate to tease me out of my shell of grief. I knew these friendships, and time, would help me to heal.

One spring morning the sun was shining and I decided I would take a walk in the beautiful countryside by the cottage. Immersed in the beauty I felt a sense of being glad to be alive, a gentle sense of healing.

I walked through an orchard, the apple trees were in full bloom. There was hardly any breeze but every now and then a petal would fall just like a snowflake. I must have been walking for hours. It was like therapy. I thought of nothing, just enjoyed the joy of nature. The heavy scent of orange blossom made my head spin. Suddenly I arrived back at the cottage. I walked in and collected all Mark's photographs bar one and put them in the drawer next to my bed. Then I picked up his jacket and put it away in the closet. I was back in the land of the living.

One Saturday Margery called on me unannounced. 'How lovely to see you,' I said as I opened the door. We went through to the kitchen where I was preparing lunch. 'Are you hungry?' I asked. 'I could eat something,' she replied. I laid a table outside in the garden as it was a really beautiful day. 'Although I'm pleased you came, you don't normally arrive without calling me first. Is there some emergency?' 'I've just come from spending a few days with Ursula in Stratford and I'm worried, she's got this new man friend and when I met him I was not impressed. When she was out of the room he made a pass at me! I just ignored it at the time but he struck me as totally untrustworthy. She's not good with relationships as you know; she's had some real disasters. Do you think I should tell her that I think he's a rogue or should I just let things ride?' 'It's difficult, because if you sometimes tell people the hard truth you lose a friend, especially when they don't really want to know,' I replied.

We sat there in the garden in silence for a while. I said, 'You know, I think she's probably lonely.' 'I'm sure you're right. You know, when she was on the stage she had so many people near her, other actors and fans that used to be thronging around her – she was often the centre of attention. She was very beautiful and was rarely out of work. She always had one admirer or another tagging on behind, just happy to be in her circle of friends. One night a man came up from the stalls and offered to marry her after the show. When you've been that glamorous and led such a full life, it's not easy in retirement to be almost totally out of the limelight, especially when you're living alone. Her only contacts with the theatre now are those silly bit-part actors at the Old Vic in Stratford-upon-Avon. It's a far cry from being a leading lady in the West End,' Margery replied.

I poured two glasses of wine. 'I suppose Ursula had many

boyfriends in those days.' 'John, she always had someone on her arm, some of them very rich and also titled men. She could have had the pick of the bunch when she was in her prime, but in the end she always chose the wrong one. She was treated very badly by some, but there was one guy that she was really in love with, they were together for a long while and no one could understand why they didn't marry. It turned out he was already married and his wife was an invalid and therefore he felt divorce was out of the question.'

'What do you think we should do about this unsuitable man?' said Margery. 'When I get the chance I'll have a quiet word with her. Maybe she will take notice of me and you won't lose a good friend,' I replied.

'Apart from your husbands, did you have any serious love affairs when you were young?' I asked. 'Well, there were one or two, but I only had one that I really lost my heart to. His name was Simon. He was tall, dark and handsome and had a charming personality. We met when I was on holiday in the South of France. I was twenty-one at the time, he was twenty-five. I was in a nightclub with a girlfriend and her brother, he was sat at the bar and appeared to be alone. Eventually he asked me to dance. I knew at once I could fall for him and before the evening was through we arranged to meet the following day.

For two weeks we saw one another every moment possible. We arranged to meet in London shortly after the holiday. For a while it was as good as it gets. Then one day he didn't turn up and he never contacted me again. I never found out what happened to him.' 'What a sad story,' I said.

'What about you, how do you feel now?' Margery questioned. 'I don't know if I'll ever recover from the death of Mark. I'm lonely and sad. I know that it's been a while, but he's always on my mind.' I told her I'd been getting letters from Joe, which always cheered me up.

'He was my first real love affair when I was in the RAF. Our affair was cut short when he was posted to the Far East because we were found out. We have kept in touch. One day maybe we will meet again but he has quite a long time still to do.'

'Why don't you try to meet someone else?' asked Margery. 'When you've had the best there's nowhere else to go,' I said sadly.

After Margery left the next day I found myself dragged back to thoughts of Joe. I decided to write to him, saying it would be good to see him.

I eventually got a reply, he had been posted to Cyprus and my letter had been forwarded from the Far East, taking several weeks to get to him. This took some time. Also the letter had been opened. I couldn't believe it: after all this time they were still opening Joe's mail. He said he would like to see me again but it would be a while before he would be in London again. He said how sad he was to hear about Mark's death and understood how devastated I was. He shared my loneliness as knew nobody on the new station and there was no tennis. I just hoped one day we could meet again.

I decided a call to Ursula was in order and she invited me down to Stratford that Sunday. I arrived for lunch and we chatted about nothing in particular. I thought a slow approach to the subject of her new man was the best course to take. After lunch we sat in her garden with some coffee. 'I hear you have a new man friend,' I said. 'Yes, he's very keen. He wants us to live together,' she replied. 'It seems a little soon for him to be suggesting such a move. How long have you known him?'

'Only about six weeks,' she replied. 'Ursula, you want to be careful. That's not very long, do you really know him well enough?' I said. 'Well I suppose not, really, but you see he only lives in digs and he hates it,' she replied. 'It sounds to me like he wants a home, and once he's installed here you'll have a terrible job getting him out if things don't work out after he moves in,' I said. Ursula thought for a while and then said, 'I suppose you think I'm a silly old woman.' 'Not at all, but I am just pointing out the pitfalls of this situation, which I think you should consider very seriously before it's too late. There is nothing wrong with wanting a relationship for companionship when you live alone, but moving them into your home opens a whole different can of worms.'

Ursula went to get us some more coffee. 'I know you're right and I should be more careful. I'm not a great judge of character, as you well know, and I'm going to take your advice.'

'I'm only thinking of you, you're such a dear friend and I

want nothing to spoil your life here. After all, if you want company all you have to do is call me and I can be here in an hour.' She leaned across and kissed me on the cheek. 'You are a dear,' she said. Soon after, I drove home, hoping that I had done the right thing and relieved that she had not taken exception to what I had to say.

I was now regularly playing tennis at a local club and noticed a new member, Jill. I remember noticing the little details about her – sparkling white teeth and clear skin. She was about my height and had a cliché of a smile, one that lit up the room. We got chatting and hit it off as we had the same sense of humour. I decided to ask her out and we enjoyed each others company. I took her out to dinner the following week and then she invited me to her house for a meal. Over dinner she shared her relationships woes, a bad marriage to a Spaniard, and I thought it better to keep quiet about mine. We played some mixed doubles at the club and things seemed to be fine. I wasn't quite sure what I was getting myself into, but I wasn't ready for a relationship with a man and it felt good to have some company. One thing led to another and soon we were romantically involved, even discussing marriage and children.

I liked the idea of having children and so we became an item, going to parties with other couples. But I soon began to tire of the bland parties and the constant questions about marriage. It was all so boring, nothing like the gay parties where everyone had a ball and there was dancing, witty conversation and lots of laughs. At couples' parties nothing ever seemed to happen, we all sat around and talked about mortgages and loans and the price of fish.

Every once in a while I had to get my fix by going to a local bar where gay people gathered. Those visits became more and more regular and although I tried to keep my relationship with Jill together I found it increasingly hard work. It was the end of the Sixties and Cheltenham was a swinging town: the Beatles, the Stones and all the top groups came there. It was a great place to be, especially if you were young, gay and looking for fun.

One winter's night I was driving home in the dark through the narrow country lanes. I was caught in a raging storm. The rain was lashing at my windscreen and it was difficult to see the road ahead. As I came around a bend a fox leapt out of a hedge right in front of the car. I slammed on the brakes but my car swerved, went totally out of control and over a grass verge into a ditch. The next thing I knew someone was lifting me out of the car. There was rain on my face as he carried me to his car and put me in the passenger seat. As I regained consciousness I vaguely recognised him from a local bar. 'How do you feel? Shall I take you to hospital? You've had a bump on the head and it's bleeding badly. Put this handkerchief over the cut, I think it best if you hold it there. It's John, isn't it? My name's Dave, I have seen you in the bar sometimes.'

'I'd rather you take me home, if you don't mind, unless you've got plans for this evening,' I replied. Dave said, 'No, actually, I haven't – I'm in no rush to go home. It's certainly not the night to be changing wheels and pulling you out of the ditch.' He locked up my car and drove to the cottage. I opened the door and asked Dave if he could find me some plasters in the bathroom. He came back and cleaned the cut and said it wasn't serious and put a plaster on it. 'I'll make some tea to warm us up. Great place you've got here.'

'At the moment I only really come here to check things out. I'm living with my girlfriend at the moment,' I said. 'Oh right, girlfriend?' he asked curiously. He obviously knew from people in the village that I was gay and must have wondered if the bump on the head had confused me.

'I thought I would give it a last try, being straight. Everybody tells me I'm mad and there are times when I think they're probably right,' I explained. 'I wouldn't dare criticise anyone, my own life is totally in turmoil. I am in the process of breaking up with my third partner in so many years. I don't seem to be any good at relationships. I have to move out by the end of the week,' said Dave. 'I always think being bisexual is more difficult because you are caught between two conflicting lifestyles,' said Dave. 'I'm finding that out fast,' I replied. 'You see, every now and then I crave gay company, it's like a fix that I have to have. Gay people can be so amusing at times and I have to say gay parties are in another league from some of the straight ones I have attended.'

Passing me a cup of tea, Dave continued, 'In the morning I'll borrow a tow rope. I already have a jack and we can get your car back on the road in no time.' 'I can't thank you enough. I know absolutely nothing about cars, my ex-partner Mark always sorted out all my problems in that direction,' I said. 'What happened to him?' Dave asked. 'He was killed,' I replied as I could feel tears begin to well up in my eyes. I still couldn't mention Mark's name without feeling sad. Dave looked shocked: 'What a terrible thing to happen.'

We carried on talking and I asked Dave to stay for dinner. Over steak and salad he told me about his disastrous relationships and I told him all about Mark and Joe. 'You never mentioned anything about your family,' I commented. 'Well, I've got parents and a brother but I never see them.

When I was seventeen I took a friend home to listen to some music in my room. One thing led to another and we ended up in bed. Suddenly the door burst open and Father came in. He pointed to my friend and said, 'You, out.' My friend pulled on his jeans, grabbed his t-shirt and escaped at great speed out through the front door. Father came back into the room and just said, 'Pack your things and get out of here.' I've never seen my parents since. At the time I was an apprentice in the building trade on bad money, I used to get up very early and do a paper round before work just to make ends meet. After a while I got my first steady boyfriend, we moved in together and it was great for a while. Then he met someone else and I was on the doorstep again. The second one was almost a carbon copy of the first and now it's happening for the third time.' We talked for hours over bottle after bottle of wine and by the end of the evening I felt like I'd known Dave all my life.

I woke up late in the morning and could smell bacon and eggs being cooked in the kitchen. I washed and dressed and went down to find Dave had also made toast and a pot of tea. I watched as he worked in my kitchen, his mop of curly black hair bouncing as he cooked. He was bare-chested, his skin permanently tanned from working outdoors.

'This is a pleasant surprise, you've been busy. Maybe I'm talking out of turn but I've been thinking, if you've got to find somewhere by the end of the week, why don't you move in here for a while?' He almost shook my hand off in agreement. I had a feeling it was going to be fun having Dave around.

The lodger

I'd been living at Jill's for a few months by now and she was becoming increasingly nervous that her parents would drop in and find me there. She told me her parents would never speak to her again if they thought she was living, unmarried, with a man. So rather than risk being found out I moved back to the cottage. Dave didn't seem bothered and moved on to the settee. Dave got me back into the gay scene, taking me to parties, but making it clear I wasn't available. Strangely my relationship continued, healthily, with Jill. I studied at college and played a lot of tennis and she liked to cook and attend the many social gatherings that happened at the hospital where she was a nurse. I knew I was gay and wanted to be with men but at this point I respected my relationship enough not to go there, despite Dave regularly telling me that I needed to get laid. Apart from my own conscience I had Margery.

We'd spent many hours chatting about my relationship with Jill and she seemed more and more concerned about how involved we were. She asked if I would go and see her in London.

I drove to her house on Friday and after the usual pleasantries she said, 'Are you still thinking of marrying Jill?' I said that I was. She then asked me if I was happy. I replied that I thought that I was. 'It's nothing like the happiness I had with Mark; this is completely different. It's more like being friends,' I said. Margery replied, 'Don't you think you're settling for second best, darling. You've been riding side-saddle for so long you have surely forgotten how to ride straight!' I collapsed in giggles then she started. It was some time before we could continue without starting all over again. 'You have such a way with words, but, you see, there is nobody on the horizon and I never go for mainstream gay guys,' I said. 'I've always been attracted to very straight or bisexual men; they're not the kind you can pick off a shelf. It's often pure luck if you are fortunate enough to meet one,' I continued.

We stopped for a while as she poured us both a gin and tonic. 'If you marry Jill and then you meet someone you fall head over heels for, where does that leave Jill? It's not fair on her if she doesn't know the truth of the matter. I guess you haven't told her you are gay,' questioned Margery. 'Well, no – I haven't yet, but I know I'll have to before long,' I replied. 'It's just that I don't want you hurt,' said Margery. 'I'm in my thirties now. I can't be that choosy. In gay years I'm old,' I replied. 'Don't be silly. You are no age and you look great. I don't want to hear any more talk like that, so take advice from your adopted aunt, even though it's none of my business.' I knew she meant well as she came across the room to kiss me on the forehead but I couldn't help thinking she really didn't understand how lonely I was.

I knew Margery wanted to do more than talk about Jill that weekend and on Sunday she announced we were off to meet a male friend of hers. We arrived at the Coal Earn in Earls Court, a notorious gay bar full of ageing gay bikers dressed from head to toe in leather. I felt quite nervous sitting in such an obvious pick-up joint so was pleased when Margery's friend, James, arrived. He looked very bohemian, quite tall and slim but rather camp with a white silk scarf draped around his neck. He was keen to take me somewhere quieter to talk and Margery made her excuses and left.

We made our way to a nicer bar where he told me about his job as a costume designer for the theatre. He promised me good tickets for all the shows. Over drinks he told me about his friend he lived with and their ten-year relationship, he wanted me to visit them in Hampstead next time I was in the city. I immediately felt a connection with this intelligent, articulate man and knew we'd become good friends.

As I drove back to the cottage on Monday I thought about what Margery had said about telling Jill. She was right, I had to tell Jill, but how would I tell her and what would her reaction be? I decided to delay the problem for a while, hoping, by some miracle, things would sort themselves out.

I found myself in Hampstead just two weeks later, after an invite from James to see the house and meet his friend, Rupert. The house was an old Edwardian building in a very beautiful part of Hampstead, initially looking far too big for the two people I knew lived there. But I soon realised they needed more space than the average couple. Several rooms were devoted to costume design and others were full of works in progress. There was one room that was full from floor to ceiling with just fabrics.

James welcomed me in and introduced me to Rupert, who was also tall and slim and was obviously very arty. He was wearing a kind of smock which was covered in different shades of paint. He was very good looking with dark hair and green eyes. 'I'm sorry about the smock, but I'm doing some designs for the scenery for King Lear,' Rupert said. 'You two seem to have the London theatre scene tied up regarding scenery and costumes,' I replied. They let me in on their plans to take me out to what they called an 'amusing pub' that evening. I couldn't wait.

Rupert, James and I arrived at this pub, which was more like a small theatre with a huge bar at the rear. The stage was small but the acts used every inch. Singers, dancers and comedians – all with unusual style and different performances – shared the stage. After two hours of the best talent I'd seen in years we made our way to a quieter bar where I filled the chaps in on my recent history. They were staggered when I told them that I was thinking of marrying Jill.

'You can't be serious,' said James. Rupert said he thought I must be mad to even consider it as he knew other friends who had done so and ended up in unhappy relationships.

It was my wake-up call. I realised I hadn't thought through what marriage or children would mean. I'd met two people I could really identify with and I knew that was the direction my life needed to go in. It finally felt like things were picking up for me.

As my relationship with Jill cooled I started spending most weekends in Bristol. A gang of us, including Dave, would go down and wend our way round various pubs, causing mischief and looking for love.

One night I visited a pub on the Bristol docks called the Radnor to see the jazz band that played there every Friday night. I was stood at the bar when a rough-looking guy asked me to make up a four at darts; I didn't want to disagree with him so played the game. Pat, the darts player, was obviously Irish. A bricklayer by trade, he lived in digs in the town and, despite his dusty old clothes, he was ruggedly handsome with long shoulder-length dark hair and the most amazing large green eyes. He wasn't much taller than me but was solid, something belied by his quiet voice I sometimes struggled to hear. I finished off my pint and was ready to go and find the rest of my crew when Pat asked if I'd like to go to a place he knew.

The club was small but very nice and over drinks he filled me in on his family back in Dublin. He'd been working in Bristol for six months in a well-paid job and was just looking for a flat rather to get out of the digs. 'I'd take you back there, but I think it would upset my landlady,' he said. I didn't know whether he was making a pass at me because he didn't appear to be gay. I'd arranged to meet the guys at 10pm and made to leave. 'Do you think you will be around next weekend?' Pat asked. 'Because if you are I'd like to meet you again,' he said, although his tone was doubtful. 'Sure, I should be in the same place I met you, the Radnor on the docks,' I replied.

I spent the next week debating whether to go back and meet him. I had no idea what his intentions were or if he even had any. When I told the others, they just laughed and said that he probably was after my money or a free night out. In the end I decided to turn up, as he seemed genuine and I didn't want to let him down. I knew I could always use my boys as an excuse to escape. Pat appeared not long after I arrived at the Radnor, smartly dressed in a new leather jacket and jeans. His hair was washed and groomed and he looked devastatingly handsome. 'Have you eaten?' he asked. I said I hadn't and he offered to take me to a club where they did really good food. 'I've had a great week, and all my horses came in,' he told me, 'so it's on me.'

Over dinner and a very good bottle of wine I tried to figure out where this was going. Maybe he was looking for a friend and company? I found out he'd come to England to get away from the chaos at home and lack of work.

'Do you have to meet your friends tonight?' he asked. 'No, I'm free as a bird,' I replied. He looked across the table with those big green eyes. Now I knew where it was going. 'I really like you, John.' I couldn't believe this macho-looking guy could be interested in me. I opened my mouth but no words came out. 'You do like me a little, don't you, John? I know I'm a bit rough for someone like you, but maybe you'll forgive me for that.' I breathed a sigh of relief and came straight to the point. 'Where can we go?' I asked. 'That's no problem, there are plenty of hotels here in the city, and nobody is likely to ask questions.' 'Let's check in before it gets too late, then I'm going to treat you to a good drink at the bar,' I said. But we never made the bar; we ended up in bed and stayed there until morning. I've heard of fallen women but I guess I was a fallen man.

My plans to stay faithful to Jill fell apart. I'd meet Pat every Friday in Bristol and wouldn't go home until dawn on Monday morning. I would have a quick shower and shave, grab some breakfast and leave for work a total wreck. Pat and I were so attracted to one another we hardly ever slept. I'd already decided that my relationships were doomed so when Pat's father died and he said he had to go back to Dublin I wasn't surprised. It was just another love that would slip away from me.

But Pat had other plans; he invited me to go to Dublin. Pat met me at the airport and booked us into a good hotel for three days. I knew I couldn't stay at his family home but he told me there was more chaos than usual as one of his brothers was getting married that weekend.

'It's going to be great fun,' said Pat. 'Twelve of the male guests have arranged in secret to all dress up as brides, and will arrive at the church at the same time as the real one.' I'd never heard of such a thing but I was enjoying the Irish sense of humour.

The mention of a wedding made me think of Jill. 'What's wrong?' asked Pat. I told him about Jill. 'You're not serious,' he said. 'I know you think I'm crazy like everyone else. It seemed like a good idea at the time, but now I think I must be crazy too,' I replied. The wedding was wonderful, filled with his family of genuine people and crazy laughter.

We had too much of everything that weekend, including sex on a scale I had never encountered before. I don't know what it was about Pat, but I couldn't ever feel sad or down in his company. By the end of the weekend I had decided there was no way I could go on fooling myself about getting married. I wondered how many people had to tell me I was a fool before I listened to their advice.

Pat drove me to the airport on Monday morning. Every time we said goodbye I didn't know if I would ever see him again, but I hoped that I would. Pat told me that it was unlikely he could come back to Bristol, however much he wanted to, as he had got a really good job in a building firm to help his mother out financially.

I told him I would make the journey to Ireland but my trips would be limited. We'd grab time when we could. Pat visiting London gave us a chance to spend a few days at Margery's house. Margery instantly fell for Pat, she thought he was charming and terribly funny. He'd play practical jokes on her and it was all taken in good humour.

She got her own back by making him think he was in a separate room to me. 'We don't allow sex here,' she said, winking at me from behind his back. He told her he was celibate and he had no experience whatsoever and maybe she could enlighten him. When Ursula arrived, Margery pretended that she had to share a room with Pat. Ursula didn't turn a hair and said it would be good to have a younger man again. I told them not to be so wicked, and that I was sure they were embarrassing Pat. More people arrived and we decided on an impromptu party.

Pat made a good impression with all of our friends. Ursula thought he was very different from the men I'd been with in the past, but that she liked him.

'He's just what I need at the moment, after Mark's death,' I said.

The party feel into its usual hectic rhythm. Margery put on some fabulous food and Rupert, in his usual flamboyant manner, said that she should have one of those cooking programmes on television, and get paid enormous sums of money.

Margery found the piano keys and we all had a singsong. Rupert and James did a hilarious take-off of 'Round the Horne', mimicking the stewards' sketch performed by Kenneth Williams and Hugh Paddick. It was one of the best parties Margery ever hosted.

What had started out as a chance meeting between Pat and I was developing into something far deeper. I knew our worlds were far apart, but it didn't seem to matter when we were together. The next morning at breakfast I found a small parcel on my side plate. 'Is this for me?' I asked. Pat said it was just a little something he brought over from Dublin for me. When I opened it, there was a beautiful wristwatch inside, with both our initials engraved on the back. It was so unexpected I felt almost sad that I never thought to get him anything. I couldn't help but throw my arms around him.

We spent the rest of the weekend in a social whirl, Pat trying on elaborate Elizabethan costumes at Rupert and James' house, eating duck in a delicious orange sauce and listening to live acts and dancing the nights away. On the final night Pat told me he craved to live this kind of life and I thought it was the right moment to give him the gold St Christopher I had secretly bought earlier in the day. He looked at our initials engraved in the back. 'What am I going to do without you?' he said. I couldn't help thinking how lucky I was to have met him.

I knew before I saw Pat again I had to tell Jill what was going on. I delayed things one more time by telling her I didn't think we could have children as we were so dependent on her income. I passed my exams at Bristol University and Jill thought this would secure the future she wanted as I could now get a better paid job in local government. I went for job after job; I was always the best qualified but never landed a position. The final straw came when Jill said she could cook a shoulder of lamb and we could live on it for at least three days.

I don't know if it was the thought of living on shoulder of lamb endlessly or the fact that our finances just didn't add up, but I knew our relationship wasn't working on many levels. I began to lay the seeds of doubt in Jill's mind about whether our life together really worked. I certainly had no doubts that the time had arrived when I would have to be truthful about the complications in my life. I thought enough about Jill not to hurt her in any way, but in the end the truth would have to be told.

I had no contact with Pat for a long time and then suddenly I had a letter. Sick to my stomach, I read the words: 'Pat and Audrey Smith invite you to their wedding'. I hoped there was a good reason for this marriage and couldn't stop myself from attending.

I didn't want to hang around after the wedding so I booked to go to Dublin for three days. Pat met me at the airport. He looked at me shyly. 'I guess it was a bit of a shock,' he said. 'Yes, after our last meeting, it was,' I replied. 'I'll tell you all later,' he said. What a cheek: he tells me I'm mad to contemplate marrying Jill, and now he's doing the same himself.

He took me to the same hotel we'd stayed in the last time I was there. In my room I wanted an explanation. 'Now, before you say anything, it's not me getting married, it's my brother,' he said. 'We only discovered the error the printers made yesterday, because we gave them a list of addresses and they took care of posting them off.' I couldn't help but burst out laughing. 'I was all ready to give you a telling off,' I said.

I looked towards the bed and his case was standing there. 'So I guess you're staying here with me,' I said. 'I thought you were coming over a long time ago,' he said. 'Well, I hadn't heard from you and I wasn't sure if it would be convenient. You only have to pick up the phone and call me,' I replied. 'You know how it is, you get tied up with work and personal problems and time goes by so quickly these days,' he said. 'You should get you priorities right,' I replied. He wanted to stop the talking. 'Come here, I've been waiting for this far too long.' He picked me up and threw me on the bed and dived on top of me. It would have been an erotic moment, but the end of the bed fell off and one of the legs snapped. We ended up sliding down on to the floor. When I got my breath back, I said, 'I've got to phone Margery to tell her about this, she'll love it.'

The boy

We lay in bed afterwards, still sloped down towards the end of the room.

'I've got a confession to make,' Pat said. 'I've got a seven-year-old son. He was conceived when I was drunk on a one night stand. I have no contact with the mother but she just asked me to look after him when he was six months old. When I was in Bristol Mother looked after him but when my father died she couldn't handle it any more. He's a great little chap and no trouble at all and I'd like you to meet him,' Pat said. I was taken aback but not horrified and agreed to take him to the park on Sunday, extending my stay by a few days.

A small dark-haired little boy ran out of the house and threw his arms around Pat. 'Are we going to the park, Dad?' 'Of course we are, I promised you, didn't I?' He then turned to me and said, 'What's your name?' 'John,' I replied. 'My name is Brandon,' he said. 'Are you Dad's friend?' 'Yes, and I'm from England,' I replied. He caught hold of Pat's hand and then mine and talked all the way to the park. It was the nearest thing to a family outing I'd had for many years. I bought ice creams and Pat produced a tennis ball so we could play catch.

At 4pm we went for tea and cakes. Brandon looked at me, seeking out the truth in a way only a child can. 'Do you sleep with Dad?' he asked. I looked at Pat not knowing what to say. Pat rescued the situation by saying that it wasn't polite to ask personal questions like that when you have only just met. 'Uncle John doesn't mind.' Brandon wouldn't be put off, so I said that we did share a room occasionally. 'Like my uncles,' he replied. 'Not quite, but in some ways,' said Pat.

'Would you rather sleep with Uncle John than your brothers?' Brandon asked. 'Yes, I would. My brothers snore, for one thing,' said Pat. At last he seemed satisfied with the explanation. 'What do you do in England?' asked Brandon. 'I'm studying to be an interior designer,' I replied. He looked baffled. 'I design the inside of houses.' 'Do you get lots of money?' he asked. 'Enough to come to visit you in Dublin,' I replied. We finished our tea and walked back through the park. I told Pat I thought Brandon was amazing. 'He's the reason I can't leave Dublin.' 'Why don't you bring him over to England for a holiday? It wouldn't cost much staying with me in the cottage.' Pat said that he thought it was a great idea. 'Do you think you could stand him being around all the time? You're not used to children,' he said. 'If I can handle you he'll be no problem,' I replied.

Over the next few days I became very close to Brandon. He wanted to know why I couldn't stay in Dublin.

'He has a cottage in England and his work is there. If he doesn't work he wouldn't have money to come and visit us,' said Pat. 'Why can't he work here?' said Brandon. 'Maybe he will one day,' replied Pat.

Leaving Dublin was horrible, especially with a distraught seven-year-old holding on to my arm in protest. 'You can come and see me very soon,' I said. And I really hoped they both could.

It was late spring when Pat called to say he could bring Brandon over at the end of June. I decided before they arrived I'd have a word with the neighbours, who had two boys around Brandon's age – they'd be perfect playmates. The day of their arrival I turned up at the airport far too early and hung around nervously at the gate. I spotted Brandon as he saw me and he ran full pelt into my arms, almost knocking me over. We were soon playing family in our cottage. I'm sure our neighbours must have thought it was strange that two men were looking after a young child, but if they did object they never said and they were quite happy for all our boys to play together. Brandon and his new buddies were soon inseparable. I knew with each day that passed I was falling more deeply in love with Pat and I started to dread their return to Dublin. I didn't want to take them to the airport; I could physically feel a pain in my chest when I thought about it. But poor Brandon insisted and we cried buckets of tears and love standing in the departure lounge. I longed to go with them and I longed for them to stay. I wasn't sure how many times I could go through it and I did wonder for a while if it would be better to cut off all contact with Pat. But then Pat would call and I knew there was no way I could never see them again.

We'd arranged for Pat and Brandon to visit at Christmas but in November I picked up the phone to hear sobbing on the other end. 'Pat? Is that you? Whatever is the matter?' I questioned anxiously. 'His mother. She's back and she wants full custody,' he sobbed. Pat explained Brandon's mother had suddenly reappeared a few weeks earlier, demanding full custody. She was quite serious and advised Pat to find a solicitor. Over the next week I spoke to Pat every night, listening to his concerns and fears about losing Brandon as the court date approached. But the worst was about to happen. The judge was a women's rights campaigner and brushed aside the wonderful care Pat had provided for Brandon, awarding his mother full custody. He told me Brandon screamed endlessly as they took him from the court.

He may have been tough on the outside but this destroyed the centre of who Pat was. He began drinking and was soon an alcoholic. He'd call me late at night, drunk, and end up crying down the phone. In the end I couldn't stand it any more and switched the answerphone on to take his calls. I thought about going to Dublin to see him, but it was clear I could do nothing to get Brandon back so I sent him a plane ticket to come to me, hoping time away from Dublin would help him get his life back on track. I turned up at the airport but he never arrived so, left with no choice, I got on the first plane to Dublin and made my way to his mother's house.

'Try the pubs,' his brother Jim suggested. They didn't seem very concerned about him although they hadn't seen him for a week. I went to every pub I could find in Dublin but there was no sign of Pat. I talked to every bartender but he seemed to have vanished. I checked with the police and hospitals, no sign. I was resigned to returning home when a local man said he thought he'd seen Pat sleeping rough in the park. I knew he was unlikely to be there during the day so I made my way back to the park after the pubs shut. And there, sat on a bench, was Pat.

He was in the most terrible state. I don't think he had washed for a week and obviously hadn't eaten in days, his face was gaunt and his skin pale and sallow. I touched him gently on the shoulder and when he saw me tears began to run slowly down his cheeks.

'Come on, I'm taking you to a hotel to get you cleaned up,' I said. I managed to smuggle him through the reception and stripped off his smelly clothes before dumping him in the shower. I ordered room service and gave him some of my clean clothes but all he wanted to do was sleep. I didn't think it was the right time for questions so I let him rest.

I had no idea where we'd go from here but at least I had found him and that was a start.

Over breakfast the next day I gently suggested we contact Brandon's mother, Mary, and try and arrange to see Pat's precious boy. 'Where does she live?' I asked. 'It's a small village five miles from here,' he replied. So I hired a car and we drove to the village, easily finding the small cottage that she rented. 'Let me go in first, maybe she won't be so difficult if she sees me,' I suggested. I knocked at the door and an attractive, very slim woman cracked the wood open an inch. 'Who are you?' Mary said. 'May I come in?' I asked. 'Certainly not, I have no idea who you are. I'm not accustomed to letting strangers into my house.' I decided there was no time to waste with this ice queen.

'I'm a friend of Pat's, and I have to tell you it is devastating his life never seeing Brandon.' Her nextdoor neighbour came out at that point and that was enough to make her invite me in. 'Come in, I don't want that nosey woman hearing what we have to say.' I explained all about the late-night phone calls from Pat, and how I had found him sleeping rough in the park.

She was amazed at the effect it had on Pat. 'I never knew he would react like that. Why didn't he contact me before? He doesn't have to kill himself over this,' she said. 'You see, they were very close when you were abroad. He really loves Brandon.' 'Where is Pat now?' she asked. 'Outside in the car,' I replied. 'Go and tell him to come in,' she said.

As soon as we were in the house it became clear Brandon's mother was quite happy for Pat to see Brandon. Pat broke into a grin I hadn't seen since the last day of our summer holiday with Brandon.

'He's at school until four o' clock. He'll be home in half an hour, you can stay and see him, if you like,' Mary said. The reunion was truly beautiful. Brandon ran into Pat's arms, I didn't think they would ever let each other go. Then Brandon spotted me and crashed into my arms. We took Brandon down to a park nearby and it was like old times. Brandon wanted to know when we would be coming again, and when he would be coming to England to visit me – as usual, he never stopped asking questions. Back at Mary's house she wanted to know if Pat and I were an item. She said she could tell by the way we looked at one another. I told her about their last visit and how Brandon loved to play with the neighbourhood boys. 'I don't mind him visiting you when he has holidays. It will give me a break,' Mary said.

As we drove away Pat reached for my hand and kept hold of it as he thanked me for what I'd done. 'You could have done it,' I said. 'I thought when the judge gave her full custody that meant I couldn't see Brandon,' replied Pat. 'Mary is very accommodating; she even said that you can both come to England to see me in Brandon's holidays,' I told Pat.

I asked Pat if he was still working and although he wasn't he knew he could get his job back. I was keen that he didn't slip back into old ways so I said I would set him up in a studio apartment and pay the first month's rent, after that it was up to him. We looked around the next day and found a really nice studio, fully furnished, in a good area in Dublin. I helped Pat move his clothes and a few odds and ends in. He was a different person from a few days ago and I watched him become strong again. I left him with a caution to watch his drinking and he knew he had a reason to stay sober.

I wasn't surprised when I didn't hear from Pat. I presumed he'd be caught up in Brandon and I had my long-neglected career to focus on. A few weeks later I had a call from Pat, saying he was working extra shifts to save money for a flat and he had no intention of moving back to his mother's. He asked if I would go to Dublin and help him find a flat when he had the money, of course I agreed. We arranged for Pat and Brandon to visit for the summer and the time soon rolled around. It was a happy repeat of the previous year, Brandon full of questions and keen to continue his friendships from the summer before. They played in the woods and often came back black with mud. Pat and I grew close again and we had another emotional farewell at the airport, but this time I was determined I would see Pat soon.

It was almost six months before I got to Dublin. Pat called to say he had the money for a deposit for a flat and needed my help. I'd been working solidly for the last six months, partly to keep my mind off Pat, and I knew I was ready for a break. The afternoon I landed he took me to a small village not far from where Mary and Brandon lived and showed me a small cottage that needed renovation. It was up for auction the following day.

The bidding started and there seemed to be only three people interested. Pat said he had been to the bank and they'd told him how much he could borrow. After a short while it began to look like it was going to be beyond Pat's limit. I didn't want him to get carried away, but I could see he had set his mind on the cottage.

The bidding finally reached his limit and one of the other interested parties had dropped out. Pat made his last bid and the other people went one thousand higher. I stepped in and secured the cottage at five hundred more. 'I can't afford it,' muttered Pat. 'Yes, you can, I'll loan you the extra,' I replied. As the auctioneer knocked down his gavel Pat grinned at me and threw his arm round my shoulder.

That evening we took Brandon out to the cottage – he wanted to know if we were all going to live there and we gently explained that we'd spend time there in the holidays. As children do, he was soon on to the next thing, reminding us that Pat's brothers would never stay as Pat couldn't stand their snoring. The cottage was a mess of rooms: two bedrooms and two reception rooms that really needed to be knocked into one, a kitchen that was just the right size and a bathroom that needed gutting.

I told Pat I'd leave the building work to him but would help with interior design. Brandon soon discovered a gem of a garden out the back and was full of talk of it when we got back to Mary's. We all celebrated together with a bottle of champagne. I was thrilled Pat was happy and secure and I knew I could go back to England without any worries about his future.

I hoped Pat would settle down into a family life and see more of Brandon. Each week he would call with an update on the cottage and I popped over to finish the interiors once the messy building work was completed. Each time I spoke to him or saw him he seemed content and at peace with where he was.

Just after my visit to finish the decorating, Pat called. Mary had suddenly decided she didn't think it was a good thing for both of us to be around Brandon as she was concerned he would work out we were gay. We'd never outright discussed our sexuality with Brandon and were unsure of how to tackle the subject, so my visits to Pat were put on hold. The threat of losing Brandon was enough for Pat to cool our relationships.

I was furious. 'In other words, Mary wants to split us up,' I said. 'Are you happy with this arrangement?' I asked Pat. 'We either do as she says or she won't let me see Brandon.' I thought that would be the last I would ever hear of Pat. It ended so quickly and threw me back into the turmoil I'd felt after I lost Mark. I buried myself in work and withdrew from friends and my social life.

Back at the cottage Dave decided I needed a few projects to get my mind off Pat. First on his list was making the summerhouse habitable. He dug a trench down the side of my garden and installed plumbing and electricity. I had a fair idea what we were doing wasn't legal but Dave had a way of charming me into anything. He kitted the place out and was happy living in his outside palace.

We decided as we'd done so well on the summerhouse we would build a conservatory on the side of the cottage. Dave painstakingly tracked down reclaimed materials that would be in keeping with the cottage, including glass patio doors with original stained glass in them. Rupert and James visited and said they had just the thing to cover the huge windows, some spectacular stage curtains. They came back a week later and carried out their drapery, creating a theatrical feeling that bought a smile back to my darkened heart.

Dave and I settled into comfortable companionship. My dog Diamond became resident on the couch in the new conservatory while Dave was constantly looking for a suitable relationship. I never asked about his conquests, but he usually came into the kitchen after one of his erotic nights of passion, always kicking them out before sunrise.

I always wondered how good they would have to be to get a pass to stay. Always the joker, Dave told me I was turning into a boring old fart and should get back on the scene. I was too afraid I'd end up with another Pat, while Dave longed for just that relationship of sex and no obligation.

One night I heard crashing around in the garden. I peered out to see Dave and his newest male companion dancing naked on the lawn. It was January, freezing cold and snowing, and they were obviously drunk. I watched as they collapsed laughing on the grass and staggered arm in arm back the summerhouse. I longed for some passion and fun but I couldn't let myself go and be hurt again.

I knew I was a bit of a bore. I concentrated on work, cooked and cleaned, did the odd paint job on the cottage, and I had no social life. Dave kept asking me to go to bars and parties but I had no inclination to go anywhere. The affair with Pat was over and it had drained me of any emotion. I certainly wasn't ready to launch myself into another one any time soon.

The last visit

Months passed and I plodded on: work, home and tennis. I wasn't enjoying life but it was peaceful. I came home one evening and spotted two figures crouched on my doorstep. I was halfway up the gravel path before I realised the two people were Brandon and Pat.

Brandon ran to me and jumped into my arms while Pat hung back like a small boy who had done wrong. 'To what do I owe this pleasure?' I asked. 'I'll tell you when we get inside,' he replied. I tried to cover my anger but I was furious. I opened the door, made tea for Pat and lemonade for Brandon. I ushered Brandon into the garden, keen to talk to Pat.

I turned to Pat. 'Why didn't you call?' I fired at him, my eyes stinging with hurt. Didn't I mean anything to him? He left me without a word for so long. He shrugged his shoulders. There was a long silence, then he said, 'She's gone off again, Mary, this time with a bloke. Brandon's living with me in the cottage we bought.' I didn't want to be sarcastic but months of pain spewed out.

'Handy, then, that I made that final bid and loaned you the last amount of money,' I said. 'I'll be in your debt forever,' he replied. 'I don't understand why you cut me out of your life like that. I know she was threatening you about Brandon but you could have at least called me,' I whispered, trying to hold back tears. 'I thought that I would never be able to see you again and it was no use to keep calling you. I didn't know what to say,' he answered.

I had no idea where our relationship stood but Pat wanted to know if I'd met anyone else. I told him I'd been far too hurt by what he'd done to me.

'Why are you here?' I asked. 'Because Brandon kept asking where you were and he wouldn't shut up until I promised him we would come to visit. Mary has only been gone a week so there has been hardly any time to adjust, she wanted me to store some of her things, I had to inform the school that he was now living with me. She left me no clean clothes for Brandon – I had to go out and buy him some things because most of his clothes were falling apart.'

I couldn't help feeling sorry for Pat and decided I would ease up on him. I started with offering to make dinner. We talked and drank wine, easing the tension between us as I prepared chicken pie. By late evening Brandon had fallen asleep on the settee. We moved him to the couch in the conservatory. 'Where do you want me to be?' asked Pat. I now felt like I could joke with him. 'If I had a coal house to put you in, you'd be in there, but as I haven't you'd better come up with me.'

He took a shower and walked into the bedroom naked, his body muscular because of the extra building he was doing in Ireland, and the attraction that had bonded us in the first place came flooding back.

He got into bed but he didn't make any demands, so after a while I cuddled up to him and we fell asleep. We were woken by Brandon jumping on us and I went down to make breakfast, starting our first day together as if nothing had happened over the past few months. Brandon soon found his old playmates and Pat and I decided to sunbathe in the garden. I bolted upstairs to change and Pat followed behind. He came into the bedroom and put his arms round me, I just couldn't hold out any longer. We'd made love like this many times before but this time there seemed extra meaning to it all. By the time we got to sunbathe it was nearly four in the afternoon, but the sun was still strong and we both drifted off to sleep.

Dave woke us two hours later and over dinner the three most important men in my life got to know each other. Pat and Dave found laughter and common ground easily and Brandon tested us with difficult and personal questions. 'Do you and my dad have sex?' he asked, almost making me choke on my potato.

'That's a very personal question for a little boy to ask,' said Pat. 'Well, do you?' He insisted we gave a proper answer. I turned to Pat and told him it was time to tell the truth. 'You see, your dad and me have been friends for a long time and we love each other very much, so we can't help feeling sexy about each other sometimes.' Brandon thought for a moment, then he said, 'I'm not sure if it's right but if Dad had to fall in love with another man I'd want it to be you, Uncle John.'

That seemed to be enough for Brandon and I become another dad to him. It was hard for me to say goodbye, especially when I knew events in Pat's life had a habit of disrupting my own. Back in Dublin Brandon's custody battle rumbled on. Pat applied for and was awarded full custody, only for Mary to reappear and win back custody from the same judge who had awarded it to her the first time. We fell back into the endless circle, Mary holding on to Brandon and blackmailing Pat about our relationship. My contact with Pat waned. And Dave was there to pick up the pieces, taking me out to evenings at the gay pub in town and private parties that only popular people like Dave knew about. Dave had a band of regular 'boys' he had sex with.

One was George, a farmer's son, with an impenetrable Gloucestershire accent. He didn't look or sound the least bit gay and would turn up at odd times of the day and night. On one of his visits he arrived at midday. Dave was out, but said Dave promised to be home at lunchtime. 'You see, I have to be back for milking at three and it doesn't leave much time if he's late,' George explained.

I had to smile at the thought of him fitting his sex in between his milking schedules. I wondered how he managed during haymaking!

I was intrigued by how this farmer's son had figured out he was gay. 'I don't rightly know, to be honest. You know how it is when there's no girls about, you end up messing about with boys. In the end I liked it, so I carried on,' George said.

Dave did turn up but at one o'clock. 'I know we haven't got a lot of time so you go into the summerhouse and strip off, and I'll be there in a minute,' Dave said bluntly. George had a smile on his face when he came out after an hour so I guess he was satisfied. After his afternoon session Dave filled me in on his other regulars.

'There is Jake the plumber, Dan, who's married, Mike the policeman, Carl the actor,' he trotted out. 'Stop there: how do you manage all these people?' I asked. Good scheduling,' he replied. 'One time I got it wrong and two came at the same time, so we all jumped into bed together!'

I had no idea Dave had so many lovers, but I thought he must fill a need in them as they all seemed to go away happy and come back for more. I knew Dave was a bit of a rogue but you had to forgive him because the good guy wasn't far below the surface.

One time when I was ill in bed, he came in, cooked me my breakfast then a snack at lunchtime and made me a nice meal in the evening. He slept on the settee downstairs just in case I wanted something in the night. He was the one who brought Diamond, my retriever puppy, into my life – a companion I adored, even if he did eat my slippers.

Sundays we would take him on long walks; he went in every puddle or pond and would love a good hose-down when we got home. In the evenings he would sit between Dave and me on the settee and put his head on my lap. It was as if he was watching the programme too.

I was always worried that Dave's fast lifestyle would catch up with him and one evening he came home with a cut on his face and bruises everywhere. 'What happened?' I asked as I mopped blood from his curls. 'I was attacked by a group of young lads as I was walking home,' he replied. 'Did you go to the police station?' I asked. 'No, it's better to just forget it. I'll be more careful the next time,' he replied.

I patched him up as best I could but I knew he really needed stitches. 'You just don't expect this sort of thing to happen around here. It's a country area,' he said. 'But times are changing, you're not safe wandering around in the dark anywhere these days,' I replied. After that Dave stopped going out at night alone, especially when we heard of other attacks. The police finally managed to arrest the culprits and Dave found his feet as the life and soul of the party.

His next big plan to get me back on the scene was a trip to Oxford to see Marlene Dietrich in concert. The show was completely over the top as Marlene changed through twenty different dresses, belting out 'Where Have All The Flowers Gone?', 'The Boys In The Back Room' and 'Lili Marleen'. We counted twenty curtain calls at the end.

We made our way back to the cottage with a few friends we'd met at the concert and Dave decided he would entertain us all with his rendition of Marlene and the many curtain calls. The party finally broke up at three in the morning and I was glad I didn't have to work the next day. Both nursing aching jaws from laughter and sore heads from hangovers we sat at breakfast the next day and chatted about arranging a party at the cottage

'You know, I've never had a proper party here, maybe we should hold one. If we do it together it won't be so difficult,' I said. I wanted Dave to invite George but he wasn't sure he could fit it round the early mornings and milking commitments. And I was sure Dave had a backup friend or three.

Three weeks later, on a midsummer Saturday evening, we welcomed our guests into our lantern-festooned garden. Twenty of our close friends dined on all the fabulous food we had prepared as the balmy air touched our pink-tinged skin. After a very long night of festivities I managed to get rid of the last guest at four in the morning, each leaving us with floods of praise and a promise of a return invitation. That event was the night I made a painful but firm decision to leave Pat behind and move on with my life.

Dave would never let me be sad for a moment. As soon as he saw my head dropping he was there with a joke or some uplifting idea. 'What you need is another man,' he said to me one day. 'I wonder if there is anyone on my list that would suit. What do you fancy – a plumber, a policeman or a vet? There are plenty of others but knowing you, you'll want to do it the hard way.' I met a few guys but nothing ever happened. None of them seemed to be quite right somehow.

I think Dave was aware how fragile I was and took to being more secretive about his relationships. I caught him one morning looking thoughtfully out the kitchen window. 'What's the deal?' I asked. 'I've met this new guy and he's just what I've been looking for and I may have to give up all my regulars just to be with him,' he replied.

'You never mentioned him before?' I half-asked. 'You have to get to know a person before you make any kind of commitment; you know my record on relationships,' he said. 'Whenever I've made one before, the roof always falls in after a while then I am left going back to a walking, talking sex machine for anyone who will have me.' I reassured him he was a very nice sex machine but wanted to know why this one was different.

'I feel he really cares that it's not just a quick fuck and he's never in a hurry to leave, he holds me afterwards. He makes tea and brings me some in bed and we talk and I really don't want him to leave.' I understood what he meant as I'd had that with Mark and Pat.

'It sounds like you've got it bad and that's so good to hear. All these one-night stands are no good for you in the long run. We're not getting any younger and it gets difficult when your hair and teeth start to fall out and you are no longer the most desirable body on the block.'

Dave roared with laughter. 'You make us sound as though we're in some kind of cattle market, and not a very prestigious one at that,' Dave replied. I wanted to know more about this man. 'Dominic, he's twenty four, medium height, dark hair, green eyes,' Dave said. Dave told me he was coming to the house the next night and he would introduce me. When I got the chance to meet him he seemed perfect for Dave, level-headed, someone who could love Dave and keep him in line.

The next morning Dave came up for coffee as usual. 'He wants to make an honest man of me,' he blurted out. 'It's a bit late for that,' I said.

'I'm not moving from my summerhouse, it's my home and I like coming up for coffee every morning and walking Diamond,' said Dave desperately. 'I think he thinks I'm going to buy a grand house for us to live in,' he continued. I told him I didn't really think the summerhouse was big enough for two and as a get-out could he suggest spending time at Dominic's, and see where they were in a few months?

Predictably Dave couldn't settle. He stumbled over giving up George and continued their weekly arrangement. Dominic found out about George. One evening in autumn I heard crashing coming from the summerhouse.

Dominic had caught Dave in the act with George and there was a terrible fight. Spilling on to the lawn, Dave tried to pull them apart and received a black eye in the process. George ripped Dominic's shirt and Dominic punched George. I ran into the garden, yelling at them to stop, and both men ran out the side gate leaving Dave clutching his bruised face.

'Come on inside, I'll get some steak to put on that,' I said. I poured us both a large brandy and he squinted out his good eye across the kitchen table. 'I don't think I'm cut out for relationships, am I?' he mumbled. 'I don't fancy murder in my garden so maybe you should cool things for a while,' I replied.

But while I was busy lecturing Dave, my own love life

remained complicated. My memories of Pat lingered and my relationship with Jill still existed, albeit a smouldering flame rather than the full-on fires Dave had.

New beginnings

One night I was at a loose end – Dave was out, Jill was away at a conference – and I decided to go out to a local hotel bar for a drink.

On the other side of the bar was a chap from the office where I worked. He came across to say hello. I knew his name was Ian. 'What are you doing in here? You must know this is a gay bar,' he asked. I replied that I hadn't really noticed as I had only just arrived. 'What are you doing in here?' I replied. 'I'm gay,' he said. 'I'm just having a drink with friends.'

We got talking and he said he had heard I lived in a cottage in the country and seemed interested in seeing how we had renovated it, as he was studying to be a builder at evening classes. I asked him if he wanted to come over the following day after work.

The next night a casually-dressed Ian turned up clutching a bottle of red wine. I gave him the tour of the cottage and he was impressed with the work we'd done.

I opened his bottle of wine and we skipped through all sorts of subjects. He told me he was engaged to a girl, despite having a gay past. 'I'm also engaged, but I lived with a friend here for five years. Unfortunately he got killed by a hit-and-run driver,' I said. The evening was slipping away and I offered to cook. I threw together pasta carbonara and we ate in easy silence. It was well past midnight the next time I looked at the clock and Ian showed no signs of leaving.

Eventually I made the excuse that I had to get up early the next morning and I asked Ian if he wanted me to make up a bed on the sofa for him. 'I'd rather sleep with you,' he said directly, with wide blue eyes that tempted me. 'I can't promise anything,' I said. But as I did I could feel my body leaning to him. That night Ian filled a gap that had been empty in my life for a long time. We slept hard and woke at 10am.

'We can't arrive at work together, there will be talk,' said Ian. 'I'll call and say I had to visit the doctor and you tell them you had trouble with your car,' I said. I thought as I drove to work that I had probably made a huge mistake getting involved with someone again, and someone I worked with.

As soon as I got home that evening Dave came up from the summerhouse. 'Did I see a strange car driving off about 10.15 this morning? What's been going on?' he asked. 'It's a friend from work,' I replied. 'What was he doing here all night, overtime?' replied Dave. I had to laugh. 'We were working out strategy,' I replied. 'What on? Which piece of his body fits yours?' he said.

'Something like that,' I replied. 'I'll bet,' he said. After a pause he continued, 'I hope there weren't any miscalculations in the strategy.' 'Well, I thought there might be the morning after, but recent communications tell me they were all correct,' I said, starting to giggle. Placing his hand on mine he stroked the back of my fingers. 'As long as you're all right, that's all I'm concerned about. I don't want my best friend taken advantage of,' said Dave. Diamond, always alert to new people and heightened emotions, wandered over and stuck his head in my lap, a sign he wanted a walk.

'You know Diamond gets anxious when a new person arrives here. He wants extra attention, shall we take him out?' So Dave and I walked the dog. He didn't pry anymore about Ian, we just enjoyed the evening air and the countryside.

When Ian came round the following evening I introduced him to Dave. He was courteous but I sensed there was an uneasy undercurrent. The next day Dave said that Ian was good looking but he felt that Ian wasn't as upfront as he should be. Dave and Ian had had a chat about travelling and Dave was bothered that meant he wouldn't be sticking around very long. I thought Dave was reading too much into it and was getting the wrong idea. Little did I know how soon I would have to eat my words. All I knew was that I was falling fast and hard for this dark-haired man.

We hardly had any contact at work. He wasn't very camp and most people we worked with had no idea that he or I was gay, even less that we were seeing each other. He would, however, have great fun winking at me at work and trying to make my blush, leading to a few comments from work colleagues about my flushed state.

Ian was it, the reason to finally face up to Jill. I was a mess inside. I already had strong feelings for Ian and knew it was unfair to keep up the charade any longer. I decided to go and see her that evening. Just as I was leaving the house Ian called to arrange dinner in Cheltenham the next evening. I must have sounded like a robot because I was trying so hard to focus on my words to Jill.

I made my way over to Jill's but as I reached the end of her road I reversed the car and headed back home. I wasn't ready for the hardest conversation of my life. The next night with Ian was wonderful, an amazing dinner followed by lovemaking I hadn't known since I was with Pat. I wondered that night whether Ian still saw his fiancée and I told him I was going to tell Jill about us.

I arranged to meet Jill in a local pub. It was a strange evening to start with, an Irish band were playing and the noise meant I couldn't concentrate on getting my words together. I stood up to leave, convinced I had to get out, just as Jill came through the door. She took one look at me and raised one of her perfect eyebrows. She already knew something was wrong.

I tried to choke back a drink but the tension between us made swallowing tricky. We were already distant and it wasn't the easy relationship it had once been. 'I've got something to tell you,' I said. 'Who is she?' Jill asked directly. I didn't know whether to laugh or cry. She didn't seem angry, just a little hurt and confused. 'It's not a she, it's a he,' I confessed. I hesitated, sure Jill would slap me or chuck her drink over me. Sipping her white wine she half-smiled. 'Well, at least I'm not losing you to another woman,' she said.

I couldn't believe the release. Jill told me she had had her suspicions for years but was never sure how to tackle the subject. Quite frankly she seemed relieved that she would be able to move on with her life and get out of what had become an unsuitable relationship for us both. So the last straight love of my life was over, although the friendship we had would remain for many years.

I felt free to pursue my relationship with Ian and we soon reached the stage where I wanted to ask him to move in with me. I was gearing myself up for the right moment when he dropped some truly shattering news. He was going to Australia for two years.

He said the plans had been in place long before he met me and he didn't want to mention anything before it became a reality. He knew things were different now but he had to follow his dream, and as much as it hurt I could understand that. 'I want you to come and visit,' he said. He wanted me to wait for him. But two years seemed like such a long time and I didn't know if I could promise to wait as long as he needed. He slipped away just when I thought I'd caught him forever.

After he went, I became very depressed; it was like another chapter of my life had closed.

A few weeks later the phone rang. It was Peter and Steven, Mark's old football pals. I hadn't heard from them in well over a year so I was surprised and very pleased to hear their friendly voices on the other end of the line. They were keen to meet up so I asked them over to lunch the following weekend.

The next Sunday was a beautiful day so we sat outside drinking cold Chablis and chomping our way through water biscuits and creamy local cheese. Peter was keen to catch up and wanted to know what had been happening in my life during the last twelve months. 'I don't know where to start, Peter. I'm another year older tomorrow and depressed,' I said.

'How are you both?' I asked. Steven answered, 'I'm officially divorced tomorrow.' 'I'm so sorry,' I replied. 'Don't be, it's been a nightmare. She got everything, the house, the car – but I don't care, I'm just glad to be free. Thank God we had no children.' 'What about you, Peter?' I asked. 'Oh, my divorce goes through next week,' he replied.

I was a bit taken aback to find out they were both getting divorces, especially within days of each other, and so I probed a little further. 'Hope you don't mind me asking, but what's going on with you two?' I enquired as politely as I could. 'Shall we tell him?' Peter asked Steven. 'We've got nothing to hide now,' Steven replied, casting a huge grin at me.

'It all began shortly after we last saw you. We were both really unhappy with our lives. We got to consoling each other and became really good friends,' explained Peter slowly, his eyes staring hard at the grass. 'Then we went on one of those away football games and we had to stay the night. We shared a room and, after getting totally plastered after the game, we ended up in bed with one another.'

'It was a shock at first, but we never looked back. After that we decided we wanted to live together. We're in digs at the moment, which is grim, but we have found a place near here we hope to move into.' Steven finished and looked at me, almost asking for judgement. Who was I to judge?

'I can hardly believe it, you two! Living together! I'm pleased for you and it will be great having you living so close. It does seem a dramatic turnaround,' I chuckled. 'It all happened very quickly,' Steven confirmed. 'Peter and I had planned a couple of days together staying at a hotel; we had both said we were going on a business trip to Manchester.

'My wife had somehow got suspicious and hired a private detective to follow me wherever I went. I don't know how, but he took photographs of us in compromising situations and gave them to her. She then telephoned Peter's wife and arranged to meet to show her the photographs. When we returned, we were both on the street. They didn't keep it quiet, and before long, everybody knew about us, so we thought there was no reason to hide in the closet, and we moved into digs in Cheltenham,' said Steven. 'Quite a story,' I replied.

He then explained part of the reason they wanted to see me was because they were planning to go on holiday to Mallorca and wanted to invite me. Although it was clear they were already very much in love with each other I got the impression the reality of being flung into a full-on gay relationship was a little tricky for them, and there were keen to take a more experienced 'mentor' along! I said I would set about finding a flight and accommodation and just two weeks later I found myself in Mallorca.

I had a one-bedroom apartment near the main town of Palma. Peter and Steven were out in the country somewhere. For the first three days I hid away in a small cove some distance from the main beach. I was pretty sure I looked dreadful – slightly overweight and very white. But after three days in the sun living on fruit, I lost quite a lot of weight and my hair became very blonde. I looked like a different person. The physical change also prompted some mental changes. I'd spent a lot of time checking out of life after Mark died. I'm sure lots of my friends thought I was a complete square, opting out of the sexual carousel they were all on. Even then the thought of catching a sexual disease was enough to scare me off. Little did we know that Aids would soon appear, making the rest of my friends approach their relationships in quite a different way.

I was fortunate to have had Mark for five years, a real utopia that was even more special now I'd lost it. I knew even if I never had the chance to love again I'd known true and deep love with Mark and Joe. I'd had two soulmates.

On the third night, and having found my body a little, I met Peter and Steven for dinner.

'It's good to see you, I'd really welcome some company tonight,' I said. So I showered and changed while they sat on my tiny balcony drinking the bottle of wine I had opened. I put on some new clothes I'd bought for the holiday, and when I appeared they both whistled at the same time. 'What a transformation,' said Steven. 'The suntan helps,' I replied.

We dined at quite the most swish restaurant in Palma, right on top of a hill overlooking the town. As we ordered our meal Peter noticed a very attractive lady at the next table. 'Do you know who that is? It's Princess Caroline of Monaco,' he said. We ended up being served before the Princess. 'Queens always take precedence over princesses,' said Steven. Over dinner we chatted about my failing love life. They wanted to know why I was so down when they visited, so I told them all about my short-lived affair with Ian and how he'd disappeared just as I was ready to move on to the next stage.

'Ah, but this holiday is helping me already. I'm beginning to feel like cutting loose,' I half-yelled. Not the most civilised behaviour in a quality restaurant, but I could finally feel the cracks in my depression, and the light pouring in from my friends and the holiday was uncovering a new me.

The next day my sad shell was in pieces, I wanted to face the busy beach and people. I put my small bag in my usual cove and walked across the headland through the trees, had a swim on the main beach and then walked back to my cove.

I noticed a dark-skinned, handsome Spaniard following me and presumed I was about to be mugged. I wondered what for as I was only carrying a towel. Maybe he thought I had money in my shoes. I ended up half-tripping, half-running my way back to the cove. I sat on the sand, shaking a little, wondering why the mysterious man had shaken me up so much. And then he walked round the trees and straight up to me. Ready for a fight, he instead offered his hand.

'My name is Rafael. I come from Madrid and I'm on holiday here,' he said in perfect English. 'Hi, my name is John and I'm from England.' It was all so formal any fears I had disappeared at once. 'I hoped you were English. It's good for me to practise the language. I need it for my work. I compere shows in Madrid,' he said. 'How interesting,' I replied, 'I'm an interior designer.' 'That's very creative,' he replied. He must have felt the same instant connection. 'Would you be interested in having dinner with me tonight?' he asked. I told him I was on holiday on my own and would welcome the company.

I had every intention of spending the day meeting new people, just wandering the beach and making conversation. Instead I found myself engrossed in intense conversation with Rafael. We started to talk and just couldn't stop, even chatting as we made our way back to our cars at the end of the day.

He told me the name of the restaurant we were going to, it was the same one that Peter and Steven took me to the night before. I arranged to meet him at eight and drove off in my car feeling a mixture of excitement and apprehension. Back in my apartment the reality of what I had agreed hit me.

What the hell was I doing going out with a complete stranger I'd only known for a few hours? I'd come on holiday to heal myself, not get involved with someone, and yet here I was again driving off down the same doomed path. I looked at my reflection in the mirror; I looked happier and more handsome than I had in months. What was wrong with chasing happiness?

He didn't feel like someone I'd only just met. His manners were impeccable and besides, he was drop-dead gorgeous. He was as close to a latin hunk as I could imagine.

The evening passed so quickly, we chatted as if we'd known each other for years. Some kind of connection was forming that neither of us could easily figure out, but we didn't really care. Rafael insisted on paying the very expensive bill. I was desperate to see him again and made no attempt to cover it up.

'I'll return the favour tomorrow night, if you feel like dining out again, or maybe you have other plans?' I half-asked, hesitantly. With a flash of his white teeth he agreed. 'I would love to have dinner with you again tomorrow and maybe we will meet on the beach.' He didn't know it, but I breathed a sigh of relief. This guy was no ordinary man: he was special, and I knew that straight away.

We did meet on the beach the following day, and every day and night after, for the rest of our holiday. It was the third night before he asked if I would like to spend the night at his hotel. It turned out to be a five-star luxury Palace Hotel. He could see I was nervous when we arrived.

'It's all right, they know you are coming. I have checked you in,' he said, reassuringly. To my amazement he had booked two rooms, with an adjoining door. I immediately offered to pay my share, but he wouldn't hear of it.

'There are people staying here who know me, therefore I have to be careful. You see, sleeping with another man is still not accepted in Spain. I have to protect my family's reputation. I live in my own apartment in Madrid, quite separate from my family. They know I am gay, but we never discuss it and I never parade it in their presence.'

I went up to my room, not knowing what our next move would be. After a few minutes there was a tap on the adjoining door. I asked him to come in, expecting a formal invite to dinner. Instead he strode across the room and kissed me hard and full on the mouth. It was as though he had been imprisoned and suddenly released emotionally.

The next morning, when I awoke, Rafael had left me and gone to his own room. I washed and dressed and knocked on the adjoining door. 'Come in,' he called out. 'Sorry I had to leave you, but it is important we are seen coming out of our own rooms. I will go down to breakfast first and you follow a few minutes later,' he explained. It all seemed a little over-cautious to me, but it was a small price to pay for a night of heaven. We had breakfast in the palatial dining room.

He told me over breakfast that friends of his family were staying at the hotel and he was nervous about being caught out. He asked if we could stay at my apartment that night. Embarrassed, I explained about my modest one-bedroom accommodation, glancing at the marble floors and expensive tableware as I spoke. Rafael was clear in his desire. 'I don't care what it looks like as long as I can be with you,' he said.

After breakfast we made our way back to my apartment. Rafael thought it was homely and loved the fact we'd have our own space and some privacy. On our way down to the beach we bumped into Peter and Steven, who were surprised to find me hand in hand with a man. I introduced them as we walked slowly down to the sand.

Steven pulled me to one side. 'Where in heaven's name did you find him? Is he a film star or something?' he asked.

I quickly filled Steven in on our meeting and romantic night in the hotel.

'You don't waste any time, you tart,' he replied.

The real Spain

Later on that day Rafael asked if I had ever been to Madrid. I told him that I hadn't. He asked if I would like to come to stay with him in his apartment for a holiday, I said that I would like nothing better. He glanced over his shoulder to see nobody was watching and kissed me.

As we lay there in the sunshine I wondered if Steven was right with his tart comment. It was only a few weeks ago Ian had left for Australia and now I was caught up in another affair. I reflected on the time I spent alone after Mark died and knew I had to take my chance with this man. It's not every day you meet your dream man.

That night we met Peter and Steven for dinner. Rafael had

plans for us – he took us off to a drag show which turned out to be one of the most colourful and hilarious men-dressed-as-ladies acts I'd ever seen. My sides were aching. Then my Spaniard took us off to a late bar, where all the waiters were half-naked. My friends relaxed and drank sangria as we watched the talented waiters return in flamenco costume and put on a show. By four we were exhausted and said goodnight to Peter and Steven.

Back at my apartment, nightcap in hand, Rafael asked to spend the next day with me. 'I would like to take you to a very special place on the island, if you are interested. It's somewhere we can be alone. It's quite a drive, but we can stay the night at a place I know,' he said. 'It sounds mysterious but very interesting,' I replied.

The next morning we packed a few things and set out in Rafael's car. We drove to the north of the island, to Cala Rajada, where we had lunch right beside the sea at a restaurant that specialised in fish. You could watch the fishing boats coming in with the day's catch. Then we drove to one of the most beautiful beaches I had ever seen. We went for a swim in the sea and Rafael pointed to a beautiful villa overlooking the bay. 'You see that house over there?' he asked. 'That's where we are sleeping tonight.'

As Rafael opened the doors I was completely lost for words: marble floors, expensive furniture and a panoramic view from the huge windows. Rafael slid back the doors to the terrace and I saw the sun shining on the water below. As he showed me round each luxurious room I wanted to know how he'd found out about such a stunning place.

'I own the villa, as it was left to me in an inheritance from my grandfather, but I don't often come here as I find it rather lonely with no company. You're the first person I've brought here. I only inherited it about a year ago,' he said, shyly. This man was definitely turning out to be more than I could have ever imagined he could be.

We breakfasted on the terrace in the morning and then went down for a swim. 'I could easily fall in love with this place,' I said, entranced by the view and the hot sun beating down on the terrace. 'We can stay here for a few more days and you are welcome to come here any time you want. We could have lots of holidays here together,' Rafael replied. We spent the last days of our holidays in the villa, days I would never forget.

As we were leaving the island at the same time, we made our way to the airport together. I was full of thanks for the amazing holiday, but Rafael seemed quite withdrawn. 'I will miss you, John,' he said. I just nodded. 'You'll come and visit me soon?' he asked. And I promised I would. There was no way I was letting this one slip away.

On the plane Steven and Peter kept asking me questions about Rafael. My mind was in a spin. Was it just a holiday romance that would fade away because we lived in two different countries? Could we possibly make it work? Steven, the more romantic of the pairing, thought anything was possible.

I'd just stepped through the door of the cottage and the phone started ringing. It was Rafael. 'When are you coming to see me?' he asked. 'How about next weekend?' he continued. It was clear the holiday romance wasn't over quite yet.

The next day I booked my flight to Madrid and wandered down to the summerhouse to tell Dave. 'Hi Dave, I'm off to Madrid at the weekend – could you look after the place?'

'Have you become an international tart now?' he asked. 'Just what have you been getting up to in Mallorca?'

I told him the whole story, from meeting Rafael on the beach, to five star hotels and the fantastic villa. Dave wanted to know all about him.

'He's an actor and presenter on television and comes from a very well-to-do family,' I explained. 'He wants me to visit him in Madrid,' I continued. 'I've never been, so I thought it was an opportunity not to be missed.' Dave said he couldn't understand why he never met anyone like that. 'If he's got a brother, remember me,' he said, laughing.

I couldn't function at work because all I could think about was Madrid. Rafael was there to meet me at the airport and we drove to his apartment, right in the centre of an expensive area of Madrid. As we went into his apartment I couldn't help admiring his wonderful taste, everything looked like it had cost a fortune. His bedroom was like a lavish film set. One wall was covered with pictures of film stars of many decades – Monroe, Dean, Clift.

After I had unpacked, Rafael explained we were free to act

as we wanted within the apartment but outside we had to be no more than friends. I wasn't bothered as long as I could spend time with him.

He wanted me to meet his family. I felt sick at the prospect.

'They are very welcoming and will put you at ease at once' he said. 'Tomorrow I will show you the city and then we will go to my parents' house for dinner.' He had the weekend planned down to the last detail, as if he didn't want me to miss a moment of the Madrid experience. Rafael came across and put his arms around me and kissed me passionately. 'We have time to make love before dinner,' he said. 'I thought you'd never ask,' I replied.

The next day passed quickly and dinnertime arrived. 'Do your parents know about me, Rafael?' I asked. 'Yes. I went to see them as soon as I knew you were coming, but someone had already told them I'd been seen with you in Mallorca.' He seemed nervous about being seen.

'This is why I have to be very discreet when I am in public; I know it is different in your country.' I told him I was careful at home, too. 'It wouldn't go down well at work if I was one of those people who ran down the street with his hair on fire,' I replied. Rafael collapsed with laughter saying that he had never heard that expression before.

We drove to his parent's house, which I knew would be very grand, but nothing could prepare me for what I was about to see. There were huge gates with an intercom. We pressed a button and a voice asked who we were. The gates opened to reveal a long driveway ending in a circular garden. There was an enormous fountain in the centre of the drive. Large double doors at the front of the house were opened by a servant dressed in uniform. As we entered, there was a double staircase leading up to a gallery. 'Your parents are in the sitting room,' said the servant.

She opened the door to this magnificent room where Rafael's parents were having drinks before dinner. 'Welcome,' said his mother. She was a very elegant lady dressed in what must have been her finest clothes. His father stood up and I introduced myself, shaking his hand.

'We hear you live in a cottage in the country, it sounds quite lovely,' she said in perfect English. 'Well, it's only tiny, but I like it very much,' I replied. 'I hope you enjoyed your holiday in Mallorca. Our son tells us you were impressed with his villa,' Rafael's mother said. 'I thought it was the most beautiful place I had ever seen,' I replied.

'I was in England for two years in my youth,' said his father, 'I went to Oxford to study and perfect the language.' 'You certainly did that. My Spanish is nowhere near as good as your English,' I replied. Rafael was right when he said they would put me at ease. I felt no pressure to impress them in any way.

Dinner was served in a banqueting hall. I hadn't realised there were other guests who had arrived and were seated around the dinner table, and I was introduced to each one in turn. One wonderful dish after another arrived, accompanied by numerous bottles of wine. Rafael squeezed my hand underneath the tablecloth during dinner, a daring act in front of so many people.

Drinking coffee after dinner, Rafael's mother cornered me. 'I hope you will come to see us again. I know Rafael thinks a lot of you, even though you haven't known one another long. He is a sound judge of character and when he makes a friend it is not taken lightly. You are the first of his friends he has introduced to us,' she said.

I thanked her for allowing me to be in their home, and for the dinner. 'I hope it will ease your minds that I am proud to be a friend of Rafael,' I said. 'Between you and me, you're a little more than just a friend of his,' she said, winking at me. I couldn't help but smile. It was clear there was no way of pulling the wool over her eyes. A little later Rafael said he thought we should go, as it was getting very late and I had to return to England the following day. When we got back to the apartment, we snuggled up together in bed and fell asleep.

Just a few hours later I was back in the cottage, getting ready for work the next day. It seemed a far cry from the social extravaganza at the weekend. Life was certainly different in Madrid. I got a call from Rafael later that night, checking that I had a safe journey. I thanked him for the wonderful weekend and said that I really liked his parents. 'When are you coming over again?' he asked. 'It's your turn to come to me,' I replied. 'I'll be over next weekend,' he said.

I spent the next week preparing for Rafael's arrival.

Everything had to be perfect after the time he gave me in Madrid. I couldn't compete with his lifestyle but I had to make everything as clean and fresh as possible, so out came the paintbrush and the cleaning materials. I even shampooed the carpets. Dave came up to the cottage, wanting to know if I had royalty coming. Running a finger along the immaculate mantelpiece, he commented, 'This guy you've met must be something else.'

'As far as looks and manners are concerned he's up there with the very best of them, and just about the most romantic guy I've ever met,' I replied. 'I'll look forward to meeting him, then,' said Dave. 'Don't just stand there watching me work, make me a cup of tea, at least,' I replied. Dave helped me after we had tea. He could turn his hand to anything and, most of the time, do it far better than I could.

When we were in the middle of bashing the rugs outside Dave yelled to me. Unable to hear him I dropped my brush. 'After all this work I hope he's not a flash in the pan,' he repeated.

'I've been introduced to his mother and father so I guess I've had the seal of approval,' I replied. 'You never know, he may turn out to be another Ian, but somehow I don't think so,' I told him, smiling widely.

'You never did tell me if he had a brother you could introduce me to,' said Dave. 'I'm afraid you're out of luck there, he's an only child!' I replied. 'It's a good job I'm known as the icon in the sack around here, otherwise I'd have nobody,' said Dave, grinning.

'I never knew I had such a hunk living at the bottom of my garden. I thought you were a fairy,' I replied. 'Bitch,' he shouted back, flicking dust in my direction. I couldn't wait for Dave and Rafael to meet.

I was there at the airport and drove him back to my cottage, where Dave was waiting to meet us. I could tell he liked Rafael at once. Diamond, never the guard dog, licked this stranger in our home on the hand. Rafael seemed genuinely charmed by my modest dwelling, somewhat of a surprise and relief after his large luxury apartment and his parents' mansion.

I invited Peter and Steven for dinner that first evening and we spent the evening like four old friends, gossiping and laughing. They had moved into their home that week, but despite still not having sorted out their things from the move, invited us to dinner the following evening. 'We may not have enough chairs to sit on, so you may have to bring your own,' said Steven.

The next day I took Rafael to Cheltenham, which he absolutely adored, falling in love with the period buildings and promenade. I had a job to get him out of Cavendish House, a grand department store. In the afternoon I took him to Broadway. He was fascinated by the antique shops and bought a very attractive piece of porcelain as a gift for his parents. We had tea and scones with fresh strawberries and cream, tucking into second portions.

Peter and Steven's house was very old and obviously in need of some love, but had a large lounge, with an open fireplace. 'It's not much, but it's home,' said Steven. It was clear, much like for Rafael and I, that the most important thing was that they were together.

They had prepared a really wonderful meal for us with lots of wine. The evening was as entertaining as the night before and it was clear Rafael really liked Peter and Steven. 'You must come to visit me in Madrid,' said Rafael. 'That's kind of you but at the moment, as you can see, we have so much work to do here. We know it will cost more than we have, so holidays have to wait,' said Peter.

A week later they received two air tickets to Madrid for a weekend break, and an invitation to stay with Rafael. Rafael had attached a small card saying the tickets were a moving-in present from both of us.

Soon all four of us were together in Madrid. After one of Rafael's shows, a talent scout came to his dressing room and asked him if he was interested in doing a screen test in Hollywood for the musical Cabaret. It would be for the role of compere. It was too good a chance to turn down so Rafael made plans to go to America, asking me to visit him when I could. I'd been here before – I didn't want the same back and forth I'd had with Pat. I began to think that the chances of settling down with anyone were very remote.

Hollywood calls

My ever-faithful friend and constant heart support Dave was once again there for me to help after Rafael left. 'How can you let someone like that slip through your fingers?' Dave gently jibed. 'You should have handcuffed him to the bed in Madrid.'

I didn't hear anything from Rafael for some time. I threw myself into work on my own interior design company, which started to turn into a real success; work flooded in from all kinds of avenues and money was no longer a problem. I was able to repay the money Mother and Father loaned me to start up.

Peter and Steven asked me to work on their house and they spent a great deal of time trying to set me up with other people. But my social life was largely at a standstill. Every few weeks Rafael would send a plane ticket and most of the time I would ignore them, determined not to get hurt again. One day a ticket arrived, travel to Los Angeles. Rafael had been nominated for Best Supporting Actor.

By the time I flew out to meet him he was a well-known Hollywood actor. He had a beautiful house, not far from Sunset Boulevard: five bedrooms, two magnificent lounges, a swimming pool and a garden brimming with exotic flowers.

Rafael wanted to take me out but, ever the gentleman, asked if I was ready for some glitz and glamour. He drove us to the Ritz, a place packed with glamour, the food only surpassed by the dancers and acrobats that came on during the main course. Sitting by his pool later that evening, a warm brandy in hand, Rafael reached out to touch my hand. 'You know how I feel about you,' he said quietly. 'Will you come here and live with me? We could have such a great life.'

Caught up in the moment I could feel the 'yes' leaving my throat. He was so romantic, and moving to this amazing place seemed within my grasp. 'When I'm alone here I miss you so much. You are probably the only real person here in this jungle,' he said. 'If you were here all the time it would make the difference. You could do your interior design here quite easily. I can see you now, 'designer to the stars' – in no time at all you would be famous'. 'I'd love to,' I stuttered. 'But it's just not that simple. I've only just started my business and I do love my home,' I said. I said I would think it over; I wasn't quite ready to close the door.

That Friday we made our way to a real Hollywood party – at Rock Hudson's house. As we drove across Hollywood Rafael told me there would be lots of stars and important film people there. I was so excited: at that time one of my favourite films was Giant, starring Rock Hudson, and I wasn't ashamed to admit I was quite obsessed with him.

We arrived at Rock Hudson's house in the early evening. The party was already in full swing. It took place around a huge swimming pool with nude statues all around. Some of the male guests looked like they spent their entire life in the gym. Rock came across to say hello, I could hardly believe I was shaking his hand. He was just as handsome in real life as he was on screen. The party got crazier as the evening went on, the men stripping off and jumping into the pool.

'This is when it really gets wild,' said Rafael, 'Shall we leave?' I nodded and we drove back to the house for a last drink in the garden.

Rafael didn't win an Oscar but he was thrilled to be nominated and it put him on the A list for future parts in the best films. The party after the ceremony was held at the house of the director of the film Rafael had appeared in, and there were so many famous people there it made my head spin. Rafael asked me to stay for another two weeks, but we agreed on one as I couldn't leave my company for longer.

I wanted so badly to leave England and be with him, and when I met him in Madrid a few weeks later I knew I should have stayed with him. He was nervous and irritable, totally different from the man I had known. When we visited his parents they noticed the change at once. His mother asked me to drop everything and go back to Hollywood with him, but I explained to her that my own business was at a critical stage.

I tried to talk to Rafael and asked him what was wrong but he insisted it was nothing. Two weeks later, in the middle of the night, I got a phone call to say he'd been admitted to a clinic after taking an overdose. I got on the next flight, filled with rage at his stupidity; there seemed no reason for him to risk his life. He had everything going for him.

I told him he was coming back to England with me and after a few weeks in the cottage with me he became the man I'd fallen for. Once he'd recovered he decided to go back to Hollywood to try and salvage his career, with my promise that I would be there whenever I could, but I knew the distance between us would make a relationship difficult.

The next night I found myself in the summerhouse with Dave, intent on drowning my sorrows in his best whisky. He tried his usual jokes but nothing could lift my depression.

'If you don't smile I'm going to throw a bucket of water over you,' he joked. I gave him a false smile. We drank till the early hours of the morning but all that I was left with was a headache. In my familiar old pattern I threw myself back into my work to escape what was happening in my love life and it seemed to help me forget Rafael.

One night there was a knock on my door. When I opened it, a tanned Ian was standing there. I shut the door in his face. 'John, open the door. I know you weren't expecting me but I need to talk,' he shouted through the wood.

Cracking the door open an inch he shoved his face sideways through the opening. 'Let me in, you daft man,' he said. I swung open the door. 'Where have you appeared from? How are things? What happened in Australia?' I fired at him. 'Slow down, John, one question at a time.' He explained, over a glass of wine, that apart from the sunshine he hadn't enjoyed Oz as much as he'd hoped and he was back here to start his old job.

'I guess I'll be seeing quite a lot of you,' he said. 'No, I'm afraid not. You see, I've started my own business and it's become very successful,' I said, coldly. 'That's fantastic, any chance of a job?' he replied cheekily. I saw a flash of the reason I'd fallen for him.

We talked and remembered the old days. It seemed so long ago. He asked to stay the night, but I told him there was no way that I was going to jump into bed with him the moment he came back, as I wanted to be free of relationships at the moment.

I told him about Rafael. He looked depressed. 'There was no way I could wait for you for over two years and I didn't expect you to wait for me, either. Life is too short. You made your choice and went to Australia,' I said, the bitterness apparent in my tone.

He finally went home and I was glad I didn't give in on the matter. But I wanted to stay friends so the next day I called him, Peter and Steven and arranged lunch for the following Sunday. Peter and Steven had never met Ian but remembered him as the chap who'd broken my heart before I met Rafael.

'I remember how depressed you were,' Steven said over the phone. In the background I could hear Peter: 'I hope you didn't go to bed with him the first night,' he shouted over Steven. 'I hope he's up to standard after Rafael,' said Steven, 'We can't have you letting the side down.' 'Well, you will just have to wait until Sunday,' I replied.

I prepared an elaborate lunch and Peter and Steven arrived

first. 'Where is he?' asked Steven. 'He has always been a little sketchy on time,' I said. 'Not a good start,' replied Peter. 'We can't have that. You will have to bring him into line. Act butch,' Peter instructed. As Peter poured wine I made introductions. I went off to make final preparations for lunch and Steven followed me into the kitchen. 'Definitely up to standard, you tart,' he joked. Lunch went down well and Peter and Steven left with winks and promises to see Ian again.

'Did you meet anyone interesting in Australia?' I asked Ian after Peter and Steven had gone. 'No one I'd want to meet twice,' he replied. 'I'll be honest with you, John. I think it was because I still had feelings for you. I know we only knew one another for a comparatively short time, but the feelings were lasting, as far as I was concerned. I did think of coming back several times, but I thought you may think I was some sort of drama queen, so I saw it through,' he said. 'You certainly didn't make it plain to me that you felt that way,' I shot back. 'Actually, you were still engaged to a girl at the time.'

'You didn't know it, but I was just about to ask you to move in with me,' I said. 'I had to go away to sort out my feelings,' replied Ian. 'Did it work?' I asked. 'The moment I got there I realised I'd made the most terrible mistake. I couldn't get you out of my mind, but I knew contacting you would make matters worse. I was dreading you meeting someone else.'

'It wasn't easy for me, Ian; I became totally depressed after you left. That's when Peter and Steven asked me to go on holiday with them to cheer me up, and that was when I met Rafael.' 'So are you still seeing him?' Ian asked. I explained he was living in Hollywood and I couldn't see us continuing as before as our worlds were just too far apart.

Ian listened intently while I filled him in. 'I have never stopped having the feelings about you, and if there is any chance that we can get back together it would be everything I could wish for,' he said, and got up and left without another word. I could see how upset he was but my problem was that there hadn't been enough time between Rafael going to Hollywood and Ian coming back into my life. I felt that it was impossible to switch my feelings on and off and I couldn't be sure that Ian wouldn't suddenly decide to go off again to some distant shore.

Over the next few weeks I spent more and more time with Ian. So when an invite arrived for a party at James and Rupert's house I decided I would take him with me. I drove down from Cheltenham with Peter, Steven and Ian and met Ursula and Margery at the door of the party.

James had erected a small stage in their largest room with a piano situated on the side. Ursula and Margery were both covered in jewels. Ursula was wearing a stunning black dress decorated with coloured stones and Margery wore a striking red off-the-shoulder number with a cheeky slit up the side. It all reminded me of the type of parties that were held in the

Twenties or Thirties. Margery played the piano extremely well, slipping easily through show tunes.

Our hosts gave us a rendition of 'Has Anyone Seen My Ship?' by Noël Coward, and Margery sang a hilarious version of 'Let's Do It'. It seemed to light up the party. Amongst the hilarity Margery found time for a quiet word. 'If only Mark were here, he would have loved it so,' she said. 'Have you found another friend yet?' Margery enquired.

Almost in tears I told her about Rafael and how torn I felt about looking after my business in England and being with him. I didn't want to live off Rafael and I knew I would miss my friends too much, but being apart from him was incredibly hard.

'And where does Ian fit into the picture?' Margery asked. I told her all about our fling after Mark died and my plans to ask him to move in with me before he flitted off to Oz.

'I sound like a tramp, don't I?' I said. 'No, you don't. There were long periods when you had nobody,' she replied.

'Is anything likely to happen with Ian?' Margery asked. 'He hopes there will be, but I have avoided it since he's been back because it was too soon after Rafael. I wanted to be alone for a while and even now I haven't got Rafael out of my system. Ian has been patient and I may have been a little mean to him but I am sure if I get too involved with him he may go off again, to who knows where.' Margery gave me a cheeky smile. 'He's very good looking. You could do a lot worse.'

Later that night after the others had gone, Peter, Steven,

Ian and I had a last drink together. 'What have we got to do to get you two together?' Peter probed. 'You had better ask Ian what his travelling plans are for the future,' I said, staring at him across the room. I knew that I was being mean. 'You know I had made those plans long before we met,' Ian replied, the hurt clear in his voice.

I put down my glass and went to my room. The night had got too much for me. Before we'd left Cheltenham I'd heard Rafael had been admitted to rehab again. Rafael's mother had called just after the clinic and asked me to go and look after Rafael.

Ian knocked on the door to my room. 'Are you going to be with Rafael?' he asked. 'I don't know, Ian,' I said. Confused and sad with a sore head from too much gin, I let Ian take me in his arms. He stayed with me all night, just as a friend.

The next evening, back at the cottage, Ian said that he knew what I was going through and if I wanted he would come with me to Los Angeles. I knew it was something I had to deal with alone, I didn't intend staying there for any length of time. I hated what Rafael was doing to himself. I had already helped him before and I wanted him to help himself to get over his addiction. I had no plans to spend my life holding his hand every time he went in and out of rehab. Ian made it clear he would allow me the time to sort out Rafael and my feelings. This time he was the one promising to wait for me.

Slipping away

I booked a flight the following day and arrived in Los Angeles on Wednesday. I went straight to the house in Beverly Hills and opened it with the key Rafael had given me long ago. I telephoned the clinic and they told me I could visit on Saturday as he had been there a while.

For the next few days I recovered from the flight and did some serious thinking. I knew in my heart it was up to Rafael to start his own recovery and I didn't know if my presence would make any difference in the long run. I couldn't stop him taking drugs unless I was watching him twenty-four hours a day, and there was no way that I could live like that.

I was terrified at what I might encounter at the clinic. As soon as he saw me he put his arms around me and wouldn't let me go. We walked out into the grounds and he sat beside me on the bench, pale and ill. There was no doubt that the drugs were taking their toll.

'I suppose you think I am weak,' he said. 'I don't know what to say, Rafael,' I replied, 'Why would you want to destroy your life? You have a wonderful house here, a dream career that you love, wonderful parents and a great apartment in Madrid, to say nothing of the villa in Mallorca. What more can you possibly wish for? Why do you insist on destroying yourself? You are making things extremely difficult for me and I thought you had learnt your lesson the last time, but apparently not,' I continued, trying to hold my anger in check. He thought for a moment. 'If you were living with me, it wouldn't happen,' he said. I felt blackmailed. I knew I wouldn't be his watcher, so I promised to help him recover that time but would not commit to a future.

'I think you should move back to Madrid, at least for a while, and get away from the bad influences you seem to have here,' I said. He looked sad. 'I'll stay here until you are well enough to come back to the house and then I must get back to my business. I have to earn a living, you know.'

He made the journey back to Madrid and I flew out to be with him. Rafael wanted to be in Mallorca so I called Ian and asked him to take care of things. By then he was working full-time in the business with me.

We flew to Mallorca the following day, hired a car and drove to Cala Rajada, having lunch at the fish restaurant on the quay where Rafael took me when we first met.

The change in Rafael was amazing after a few days. He looked just like his old self. We swam and sunbathed, ate lots of wonderful meals. He began to smile again and the romantic setting brought back the memories of our first visit. His latin looks and the magic of the place were an intoxicating mix. I couldn't help feeling the same affection that I used to feel when we first met. I found it impossible to resist and began to fall for him all over again.

I imagined us living there permanently but I knew it was an illusion that would disappear when reality hit. The temptation to run back to this paradise every time there was a crisis in Rafael's life would be too much to resist.

I knew I couldn't keep my life on hold. As the end of our time there drew near I didn't know how to say goodbye. I knew there was a possibility I may never see him again. Just one more overdose and he could be gone forever, and I made him promise to call me every week to let me know he was all right. When we parted he embraced me, which he never did in public. He took my hand and placed the key to the villa in it, closing it tight. His last words were, 'Come and live with me in Los Angeles.' We both had tears in our eyes.

I didn't hear anything from Rafael for over two weeks. Frantic with worry I called his mother, who sounded as concerned as I was. She asked me once again to go to Los Angeles to look after Rafael. After another sleepless night I got up at dawn. Although there had been a heavy fall of snow and the temperature was below zero, I put on my leather jacket and went out into the icy morning. Maybe a walk in the crystal clear air would help me make some sense of my life.

As I made my way through the country lanes it was as though I was the only person in the world, as mine were the only footprints in the virgin snow. Icicles had formed on the branches of the trees, and as the sun rose into the clear blue sky they sparkled like giant crystals. It was as though someone had placed them there.

The snow-covered countryside hid the imperfections of what lay beneath. I thought it was rather like my life: I had covered up the truth of the love that I felt for Rafael with materialistic ambitions, like my business venture. It was true that I didn't want to live off Rafael but now my business was running smoothly I was at last financially secure. I felt ashamed of myself for not having abandoned everything to live with my lover.

As I gazed across the snowy fields, the realisation that I couldn't go on this way hit me. I walked back down the frozen path and found myself making tea in the summerhouse. I took it through to Dave's bedroom. He had been firm asleep and he woke up with a start as I sat on the side of his bed.

I told Dave that I had decided that I would be leaving for Los Angeles that very day. He assured me that he would look after things, including Diamond, for as long as I wanted. I telephoned Ian and he promised to manage the business indefinitely as long as I would come back for a few days now and again.

As I threw the essentials into my case I knew that I was doing the right thing. Ian drove me to the airport, I bought a ticket and two hours later I was on my way.

I took a taxi from the airport to the house. All I wanted was to see that Rafael was alive and well. The house was a mess, it looked like it hadn't been cleaned for weeks. I found Rafael sleeping late after a heavy day of filming. He held me as if I would try to escape and I knew this was where I should have been a long time ago. I felt as though I was home at last.

After a few days, when we were alone in the garden, I wanted to know how all the drug-taking started. He told me he had been cast as an addict and the director told him he wouldn't be able to play the part with no knowledge of how it felt to take drugs. The film was so successful he was cast in a similar role and eventually found he couldn't kick the drug habit.

Things seemed to be great for a few weeks, then one night Rafael didn't come home. At three in the morning a taxi drew up outside the house. I had to practically carry Rafael into the house. I had no idea what to do so I called a doctor. He came down an hour later, shrugged and told me to let him sleep it off.

Rafael's promise that things would be different if I lived with him turned into a daily lie. Although I had said that I wouldn't stand by and hold his hand every time he went in and out of rehab, the reality was that this was just what I was doing. I could feel the devastation as our love was destroyed by the addictive monster that haunted Rafael's life. I tried so hard to chase it away with every weapon I had but I was dragged down to the depths as Rafael lost control of all reason to live a meaningful life.

Two months later I got a call from Ian. My business was in real trouble and he asked me to return for a few days to sort things out. I told Rafael I would be back soon. He pleaded with me not to go but I knew that I had to. I needed room to breathe.

Less than a week later I had a late-night call from Rafael's mother to say that he had died from an overdose. I knew it might happen but nothing could prepare me for the final news. I was devastated. She asked me if I would go to Madrid as the funeral would be held there and help sort out his belongings in Madrid and Beverly Hills as they couldn't face the task. I knew that I could not possibly refuse.

Rafael's mother said that it would be a good idea if I stayed in the flat in Madrid and the house in Beverly Hills while I was dealing with his private belongings. I don't know how I got through the funeral.

After the funeral I called on Rafael's parents. I was ushered into the same room where we first met. 'We have something to tell you,' his mother said. She continued, 'Rafael has left you an inheritance. He made it quite clear in his will that you should have the villa in Mallorca.' I was stunned. 'He told us that the time there with you was the happiest time of his life and that he knew that you would never forget him, especially when you were there.' She handed me the deeds and other documents. She took my arm and walked me into the garden as the tears spilled down my face. All the grief that I had been holding back since the funeral swept over me.

I flew to Los Angeles and collected Rafael's personal belongings and put the house on the market as his parents had instructed. I called Ian and told him that I was flying back to Madrid and then I would return as soon as it was respectable to do so. At a final dinner with Rafael's parents his mother gave me his watch and ring and a huge cheque for my expenses. I tried to refuse the cheque but they insisted that I took it. They said they would keep Rafael's flat so that I could stay in it any time that I wanted to visit.

When I finally got back to Heathrow Airport, Ian, Margery and Ursula were waiting for me. 'This is quite a reception,' I said. 'We have come to cheer you up. We are all going to my house for the weekend. I have booked for us to see some great shows and have dinner at the Savoy, and no doubt we will have tea at the Ritz,' said Margery. My friends knew just what I needed. Although the weekend was wonderful it made me realise I knew I had to clear the air with Ian.

I told Ian that there was no way I could go through a tragedy again, and it wasn't fair for him to be hanging around waiting for me when I couldn't promise him anything. He just smiled and said he wasn't going anywhere. He was happy just for us to be friends and he wouldn't make any demands of me.

After that weekend we continued to work together. It was a strange time but we seemed to become closer as time went by.

One day a rather odd client came into the office. She wanted us to design the interior of her Art Deco house. When we first saw her Ian and I could hardly contain ourselves. She was wearing a huge pink hat with flowers all over it and a pink veil coming down over her face. She had an oriental dress on with a split right up to her thigh, fishnet stockings and a huge handbag covered in rhinestones. We were sure she was trying to be trendy and different, but the result was hilarious.

We both thought she was probably in her sixties but she wore so much make-up it was hard to tell. Worse was to come when she described what she had in mind for the house. Mrs Portman Blithe planned on a pink and green kitchen. Things went downhill from there. Ian said, when she had gone, that this would be a challenge.

The first week at Mrs Portman Blythe's house went by without incident. On the Friday, a florist's van came up the drive. A man got out and placed a huge bouquet of red roses on the table in the hall. Mrs Portman Blithe appeared, still in her see-through nightgown with absolutely nothing underneath. On reading the card, she shrieked, 'Oh, they're from darling Donald!' We couldn't contain ourselves another moment. She must have heard but didn't say anything.

As we were packing up after work, a silver open-top Rolls Royce entered the driveway. Mrs Portman Blithe appeared on the balcony in the same see-through nightgown, waving furiously. 'Donald, darling,' she called in a falsetto. 'Daphne, darling,' replied the very English-looking gentleman.

In a completely unprofessional manner we left the house in hysterics. On Monday we were treated to a repeat performance and every weekend afterwards until the work was complete. However, we soon found out the love between Donald and Daphne was rather staged.

We noticed that both the postman and the milkman ran up the drive and then ran back again. We thought they were either trying to finish early or they were overly keen on their work. But a neighbour told us that Daphne had been caught in compromising positions on the stairs with both of them in the past. We were concerned that Daphne might take a fancy to us.

One day I bought two Greek urns with naked men in various poses as decoration. They were quite magnificent. Daphne came back from a shopping trip and, stepping out of her car, she shrieked, 'Oh, Mr. John – your urns are a poem.'

She was certainly a larger-than-life lady but you couldn't help but like her in a strange sort of way. We didn't know it at the time but she filled our order book for several years afterwards. She knew some very rich people and recommended us to them all. She was the reason our business grew, allowing me to focus on design work and, over the next few months, to branch out into commercial work.

It had been almost two years since Rafael died and during that time Ian and I had become very close. We never tired of each other's company but remained just friends. I stayed in contact with Rafael's parents and they invited me to spend Christmas with them in Madrid. I hadn't taken a holiday in that two years so I gladly accepted their invitation. I asked them if I could bring Ian and they said it would be fine and we could use the apartment.

When we arrived at the apartment it had been completely redecorated and there was all new furniture, including a new bed. I was relieved and a little sad but wasn't surprised by the thoughtfulness of Rafael's parents. The following evening was

Christmas Eve and there was to be a big party at their house. Rafael's parents seemed to like Ian and asked him all kinds of questions during dinner.

There were friends of the family that I had met before and they all seemed genuinely pleased to see me. After dinner Rafael's mother took me into another room for a private chat. She got right to the point. 'Now, I think two years is long enough to grieve. All you seem to do is lose yourself in work. It's time you started living life to the full again. I know Rafael would think so. What about your friend Ian, is he a possibility?' she asked.

'To be honest, I have been avoiding any kind of relationship. The two times in my life I have been lucky enough to have a meaningful relationship both partners have died. I don't think I could go through it again, but Ian is a wonderful friend,' I replied. 'What are you waiting for? He's very handsome.' She gave me the wink that she had done so long before when she accepted the fact that Rafael and I were lovers.

'You have never been to your villa in Mallorca since Rafael died,' she said. 'I can't bring myself to go there, even with Ian,' I replied. 'What I suggest is that you completely change everything inside and put all new furniture and soft furnishings in so that it looks a completely different villa,' she suggested. 'You are a specialist in that field. It will be exciting and fun for you to do. My husband and I will make arrangements to remove all the existing furnishings so that it will not be painful, then you can start afresh and enjoy the wonderful place.' I thought it was the best Christmas present I could have received.

We had a quiet Christmas Day with Rafael's parents. They gave us beautiful sweaters and we gave them china. When I told him about the plans for the villa he thought it was a great idea and became very excited about the prospect. On Boxing Day we went as a group to put flowers on Rafael's grave. I found the company upsetting and returned to the graveyard alone later that day.

As I walked up the path of the cemetery it seemed I was the only person there. Freezing fog shrouded the gravestones and as I approached the grave where Rafael was buried I felt the cold seep into my bones. I wished I hadn't come back alone.

I began to think about the last time we said goodbye at the airport in Palma. Tears streamed down my face and I found myself on my knees, hugging the gravestone. As stones dug into my knees I couldn't bear to think of Rafael buried underneath the ground in this godforsaken place.

I tortured myself with the idea that if I'd gone to live with him before the addiction began I could have stopped it. But I couldn't watch him twenty-four hours a day. Deep down I knew I couldn't have stopped his drug-taking or overdose. He was already hooked on them the first time I came to see him in Hollywood, I just didn't want to face it.

I stayed at the graveside until I couldn't feel my hands or

feet. All cried out, I felt empty inside. I was exhausted and I don't know how I found my way back to Rafael's flat. Ian was waiting for me. He took my cold pale hands and led me to the bed. Undressing me. he laid by my side, stroking my hair until I feel into a deep sleep.

Last chance

I hadn't heard from Joe for a long time. It was strange, but no matter what had happened in my life since we were together in Germany I had periods when I couldn't get him out of my mind. His letters would arrive from time to time and we never lost touch. Then one morning I received a letter saying that he was thinking of coming out of the Service. I was surprised as I thought it was his whole life. I had thought when he got posted to the Far East it would make him think about coming out, but it never did.

I still had to be very careful when I wrote to him to make sure there were respectable periods between communications. We were never sure whether they were opening letters between us. I got the impression that he was living his life like a monk. One slip and he would be court-martialled. He was lucky the first time but there was no Commanding Officer who was a tennis fan to save him if there was trouble again.

Each time when I wasn't involved with someone my thoughts were with Joe. I guess that I never really got over him and it seemed to me that had it been possible for us to be together, it would have been a lasting relationship. I didn't regret the years with Mark, Pat and Rafael but I still held on to the idea of a relationship with Joe.

As the time for his release came nearer he called me and said he would like to meet me. I was not involved with anyone at the time so I said it would be great to see him again. I thought a London hotel would be a good idea, two separate rooms and no pressure for any romance. I had to play it cool.

On the day we were to meet it suddenly went through my mind that this could be a terrible mistake. I was in a panic. I thought he may have lost all his hair. He may have aged really badly. I might not fancy him anymore. All sorts of silly things kept going through my mind.

I took a tranquiliser but all it did was make me sleepy. Then I took some glucose to pep me up a little. I don't know why, but I had never been so nervous in my life. I made sure that I would be at the hotel long before Joe so that I could shower and make myself look as youthful as possible.

Ten years had played havoc with my looks. I tried on a suit, it seemed far too formal. I looked as though I was going to the office. I then progressed to jeans and a sweater. That was far too casual. I finally put on a casual pair of trousers and one of my trendy shirts.

We had arranged to meet in the bar at around seven to have a few drinks.

I went into the bar at 6.45 and ordered a brandy. Nothing else could possibly help, I needed desperate measures. Several times I turned around expecting him to be standing there but it was always someone else. I finished my brandy in about five seconds and ordered another. I knew if I carried on at that rate I'd be totally pissed by the time he arrived. I took deep breaths, telling myself to inhale and exhale. In the middle of an inhalation he appeared. I nearly choked to death but recovered enough to shake his hand.

It was a good job I had prepared myself, as one glance told me he looked even better than ten years before. I was in shock. I was telling myself to keep quiet and let him do the talking; I didn't want to say anything stupid. Problem was he didn't say anything. We just stared at one another for a long time. The poor waiter waiting to take our order hovered like a bee around a honey pot.

Finally I spoke, dry-mouthed. 'Joe, it's so good to see you,' I said. 'I need not say how good it is to see you,' he replied. 'Can I buy you a drink?' I asked. We chatted for a while and it was clear that nothing had changed between us. It was like yesterday that we were together in Germany. We had a great evening talking about the old times.

'I wonder if that small hotel by the lake is still there?' said Joe. 'Maybe we could go back there sometime,' I replied. At this point I was wondering if it had been such a great move to have separate rooms, but somehow I thought it would be immoral to jump into bed together the first night. I said nothing to Joe, but by the looks I was getting from him, I didn't think it would be long before something would happen.

We both went up to our separate rooms like two good little boys but I knew that would never last and sure enough there was a tap on my door within a short time. I opened it but it was the maid wanting to know if she had left enough towels. I got into bed rather dejected then there was another tap on my door. I opened it.

Joe looked at me for a moment and then picked me up and carried me to the bed. We got so excited at one stage we fell out of bed on to the floor. In some circumstances that would have ruined the sex, but I don't think anything would have stopped us that night. For the next few days it was as though we had turned back the clock.

I had only booked in for one night and each day I had to extend the stay. In the end I asked Joe to come home with me. I had no idea what Ian or Dave would think but they were supposedly just friends. Within a few days of Joe arriving Ian told me it was obvious I had strong feelings for Joe and he wouldn't get in the way. Joe and Ian soon became good friends.

Joe and I hadn't discussed what had gone on in my life since we were last together. He never asked and I didn't volunteer my past. I briefly mentioned the villa but did not tell him how I had come to own it.

Dave was intrigued by Joe but if I'd brought back Father Christmas that would have been all right. Joe had been staying with me for over two weeks when he said that he would have to visit his parents. They were now living near

Chester and he said he would go by train. 'Do you want me to come along?' I asked. 'No,' he replied. 'You see, my parents have no idea that I'm gay and at their age it's not what I want them to be concerned with.' He went alone and I said I would meet him in Mallorca in two weeks.

As soon as he'd gone I missed him. The thought of being parted again for any length of time seemed a waste after ten years without seeing one another.

I had the feeling that if we did decide to live together it would definitely be the last chance for both of us to have a meaningful relationship. But I was getting ahead of myself. We hadn't discussed a relationship yet – it was too early days. But the thought of us being a couple again made me so happy. I wanted my soulmate back in my life. My friendships with Dave and Ian were great, but just that: friendships.

I was at last ready to settle down with someone. Whether Joe was I had no idea, but I did know he was fed up with travelling the world.

I called Margery and Ursula and told them what had happened. Both of them screamed at the other end of the phone. Margery said that it was like Brief Encounter with a happy ending. Ursula said it would make a wonderful drama. Margery said she would like to meet Joe. I told her that she would soon as I wanted both of them and our other London friends to come out to the villa in a few weeks' time.

I got to the villa a few days later and realised I had a lot of work to do if it was going to be full of people. While Joe was at his parents' house I needed time to organise the new furniture and make sure everyone had a bed to sleep in. Margery said she would sleep on the floor but I assured her no lady I knew would be doing that.

When I was doing my packing I took the photograph of Joe and me from beside my bed and put it in my case. I had treasured it all through the years and often looked at it, wondering if we would ever meet again. It seemed incredible that a glimmer of being together forever was shining. Mallorca felt like a new beginning and I wanted the villa to feel like a home.

I couldn't always be optimistic about my future with Joe. Margery said she thought everything would be fine but I was sure there were some skeletons in the cupboard. After all, Joe had said practically nothing about the ten years we were apart and I had not disclosed anything about my colourful life. She told me I was being a pessimist but I knew that in personal relationships sometimes things can go wrong even in the best of circumstances.

Joe arrived in Mallorca before the two weeks were up as he missed me and couldn't see the point of staying away any longer. The first night in Mallorca we decided to lay the last ten years out. 'You go first,' I said as we sat on the terrace.

'I had no personal contact with anyone for five years and then I met Julie, who was married to a brute of a sergeant and lived in married quarters. She played social tennis at the weekend. Her husband George had no interest in anything she did so he was never with her,' Joe said. 'I had joined in the tennis because in Aden, where I was stationed at the time, there were no real competitive games that I could take part in.

'We started talking and she seemed a really nice person. She told me her husband beat her and she couldn't wait to leave him. I never knew who told him that we had become friends, but one night he came after me when I was in civilian clothes down in the town and there was an ugly confrontation. Blows were exchanged and I ended up with a black eye.

'She disappeared shortly afterwards and was never seen again. My next encounter was with Harry, who was working at the WVS store. We had a short fling for a while. I took something back to the shop that was defective and we got into an argument. but in the end just burst out laughing.

'I asked him out to dinner and he took me to a gay club. For the time it was quite outrageous. There were transvestites, cross-dressers and all kinds of people there. The music was really good and we danced for hours. In the end we checked into a hotel and this became routine. It was nothing more than physical attraction but it satisfied a need in me for a while. At the time I was in England but suddenly he went overseas to work and that was the end of it. It's not much to tell for ten years; I lived for your letters,' he finished.

I told Joe about my life – about Mark, Rafael and Pat. He thought it was so sad that both Mark and Rafael had died but did not seem bothered that I had relationships during the time when we were apart.

He said that neither of us really knew if we would ever be together again, and we couldn't stop our lives on the offchance. Glancing back at the villa Joe looked peaceful and happy.

'I could live here for the rest of my life,' he said. 'That's what I said when I first saw it,' I replied. Rafael's parents had bought us a bed and the refrigerator was stocked with food but other than that there was nothing, but that's how I wanted it. I didn't want any trace of the trappings that were there before.

The next day we drove into Palma to an enormous furniture store to buy all the rest of the furniture. We were served by a young man who looked like a cross between Larry Grayson and Dorothy Squires. He was flapping around the store dressed in the most inappropriate clothes, a velvet shirt in dark purple and white tight-fitting trousers with flares. He wore masses of bangles and beads. I was amazed his employers hadn't said something to him. Then we realised he really knew his job. He saved us hours of time with his advice, he had extremely good taste and as soon as he knew the kind of things we liked he'd lead us to them.

His name was Miguel and he spoke perfect English so I didn't have to struggle with my Spanish. In the end we got chatting and told him where the villa was. 'Ah yes, I know it. That's the area where my family live. I go there to visit often.' he said. I told him he'd be welcome to visit.

'Oh, that would be such fun!' he said, waving his arms

about like a windmill. 'We have friends coming over from England in a few days and I'm sure we will have a party,' I told him. 'They are arriving next Saturday evening if you would like to come along,' I replied. I thought Margery and Ursula would have great fun with him.

The furniture arrived on Thursday in a large white van. Inside the van was Miguel. 'I thought I'd come to help,' he announced. 'An extra pair of hands is always handy moving furniture around. It's my day off, so here I am.' At the very last moment they unloaded a beautiful white grand piano. I said that I didn't order it, but I looked at the paperwork and saw Margery's name, with a note saying, 'This is a little moving-in present.'

'These are the kind of friends I have,' I told Joe proudly. 'We can have a wonderful musical evening,' Miguel clapped. 'Can you play?' I asked. He opened the piano and gave us a tune while it was still in the driveway. Miguel seemed to instinctively know where things should go.

That evening our guests – Rupert, James, Ursula, Margery, Peter and Ian – arrived. We heard them pressing the horn as they approached. It was chaos for a while with kisses and shaking of hands. When everyone had settled in we lit the barbeque, opened the champagne and sat on the terrace watching the sun go down. As predicted Miguel immediately made friends with the ladies and he and Margery gave stunning renditions of various musical numbers.

Halfway through the evening, as Ursula gave us her version

of 'Big Spender', there was a ring at the doorbell. I went to open the door and Diamond my dog jumped up at me, nearly knocking me over. Recovering, I spotted Dave, who was standing there smiling. I hugged him. 'There was no way me and Diamond were going to miss this party so I got a passport for Diamond from the vet, booked a flight and here we are. I don't mind sleeping on the couch, I know you've got a lot of guests,' he said, in his usual casual way.

When I managed to get Joe alone on the terrace I wanted to know where we stood. 'Do you still think you will want to marry again some day?' I asked. 'Never,' he replied. 'I'm out of the Service now. I can have any relationship I like, without being spied upon,' he said. 'What about you, have you ever wanted to marry?' 'I've had four serious relationships in my life: Mark, Rafael, Pat and you. I suppose that's a lot over a period of thirteen years. Most people are lucky if they would have had two. Where do you think we will go from here?' 'I'd be happy to just stay here with you forever,' said Joe. 'Wouldn't that be like checking out on the rest of the world?' I replied.

'I've seen enough of the world to know that if you haven't got someone with you that you love, it doesn't mean a heap of beans.' 'I guess you're right,' I replied. And it was done, our agreement to spend our lives together. We talked about dividing our time between the cottage and the villa. It seemed I wasn't a loser in love after all. Joe wandered back to the party.

As I was thinking of going up to bed Margery appeared. 'I

thought you'd be out here,' she said. 'I was thinking of going up but it's such a wonderful night it makes you feel as though you are wasting it by sleeping,' I said.

She walked across the room and poured us some drinks. 'Do you remember the time we first met in the Haven Hotel, what fun we had?' she said.

'I never thought then that I'd be sitting on your terrace in Mallorca all this time later,' she continued. 'You haven't always been lucky with your relationships,' said Margery. I nodded in agreement.

'Mark was my soulmate, but he wasted a lot of time not knowing what he really wanted. Do you remember how confused he was when we were at the Haven? You know we had five great years together before he got killed. Then there was Pat, he was one of the most sexy guys that I ever met. We had something special for a while,' I shared. 'Tell me about Joe,' said Margery. 'He was married when I first met him. I was in Germany, and we played tennis together. His wife was sleeping around with other airmen. One night he asked if I minded if he came into my bed, and the rest is history. I was only eighteen at the time and it was difficult to be gay in the Forces. He was the first person I had a proper relationship with and we got careless. He was posted to the Far East to avoid scandal – it could have been a lot worse.

'When we met in London it was like we had gone back to ten years ago.'

I wanted to know what had happened to Cecil and the

yacht. 'He's now found a much younger woman, I'm glad to say. In the end I couldn't possibly cope with him, he wanted sex every night!' she said.

As I sat there with one of my oldest friends I knew how lucky I was to have true friends and love.

'I think you had better put Joe on your party list because I intend to hang on to him this time round,' I said.

Margery made her way upstairs and I still sat there gazing out over the moonlit sea. I wondered what life had left in store for us. Would Joe and I live happily ever after or were there more twists in my tale? As I looked up into the darkness the sky was full of stars. I couldn't help thinking that somewhere up there Rafael was smiling down on me.

www.ingramcontent.com/pod-product-compliance
Ingram Content Group UK Ltd.
Pitfield, Milton Keynes, MK11 3LW, UK
UKHW041944190726
13854UKWH00004B/1789